THE JOY OF BEING A CHRISTIAN

A Collection of Sermons

Professor William W McBryde

Emeritus Professor of Commercial Law
University of Edinburgh

Printed & Published by
For The Right Reasons,
60 Grant St Inverness. IV3 8BS
E: fortherightreasons@rocketmail.com
Tel: 01463 718844 or 07717 457 247

Preface

David Cargill, the Covenanter, before he ascended the ladder to the gallows where he was to hang, is reported as saying: "Lord knows I go up this ladder with less fear and perturbation than ever I entered a pulpit to preach." It is a tremendous responsibility to preach the word of God and anyone who does not have more than anxiety about that, should not be attempting the task. Even more daunting is to expose the words to the permanency of print and the scrutiny of a wider world.

Yet, there is a well known ephemera in the spoken word and sometimes a careful and more leisured reflection can assist long term understanding. The variety of opinions in Christian literature is proof enough that no author can constantly express views with which all will agree. But that is not the point. Those who react against what is said may deepen their understanding of their own position. If an opinion is wrong, the benefit to the reader is, in John Stuart Mill's words, "the clearer perception and livelier impression of truth, produced by its collision with error." But "right" and "wrong" in this context have to be used with care. Even a faint acquaintance with the history of Christianity will show that what was generally believed to be "right" in one age can be condemned as erroneous in another.

The author has read widely and the text is lightly footnoted to indicate some of the scholarship, usually relatively recent, which is behind the statements made. From time to time there has been a gap between biblical scholarship and what is preached every Sunday. If there is any encouragement to go and look at what others have written, this book would have been very worthwhile.

Every author is very aware of fallibility and there are inevitable mistakes in the likes of references, for which apologies are made. But the substance of what is said is what matters. The messages of the Bible are what our troubled secular world needs to hear.

Bill McBryde
Inverness
November 2016.

TABLE OF CONTENTS

1. Happiness

Psalm 1:1-3
Psalm 119:1-16

In Psalm 119 the first two verses are: "Happy are those whose lives are faultless, who live according to the law of the Lord. Happy are those who follow his commands, who obey him with all their heart."[1] Psalm 119 is about one of the lessons of faith, which is belief in, and trust in, God. But it is also about teaching and about learning. It reflects what is in Psalm 1 which tells us the secret of happiness. Psalm 1 says that happy is the one whose delight is in the teaching of the Lord, meditating on his teaching day and night. Similarly Psalm 119 starts by saying that those who live according to the law of the Lord are happy. A dour Christian is a contradiction in terms. Later in verse 9 it asks a very pertinent question. How can the young keep their way pure? And the answer is to obey the Lord's commands.

Not that many of our young seem to believe this. For a start they confuse happiness with pleasure. What is assumed in our materialistic society to make people happy? Some retail therapy, eating food, getting drunk, fashionable clothes, a good holiday, acquiring the latest electronic gismo and downloading the most recent

---

[1] Good News Bible: Ps.119:1-2.

software. Yet many find that there is a temporary fix in spending money. And the addict has to continue to spend, and to try to be "up to date". Last year's model is not "cool". The advertisers make sure that we never think that we have sufficient. Nowadays we are all treated as "consumers". Our purpose in society is to spend and if we do not, the economy suffers. And those who supply us with goods and services have targets to meet and become stressed out trying to comply with them.

When asked what their philosophy is in life, one answer of the young is to suggest that they can do what they like, have fun, provided that they do not harm others.[2] But note what this may entail. The classic seven deadly sins are irrelevant in their lives. Let us go through one list of them. Pride: humility is for wimps. Envy or jealousy: of others and their status or possessions. Anger: perhaps at the way other people have reacted and anger can lead to bad temper, quarrels and grudges. Sloth: or not bothering to get out of bed or failing to work hard or doing nothing; wasting a life. Greed: the more money the better. Gluttony: a very close relationship with food. And, lastly, but not least, Lust: and lust can produce corrosive promiscuity.

---

[2] See Christopher Jamison, *Finding Happiness* (2008) pp. 51-52. This book inspired this sermon (some of its ideas have been copied in this and the previous paragraph). See also his *Finding Sanctuary* (2006).

Ignoring all, or most of, these sins in your daily thinking will lead to a very self centred and discontented individual who will never have enough.

There is also a more fundamental problem. If happiness is the main goal in life, as for most of us it is, it should be the promotion of happiness of the human race in general. The happiness of society is important.[3] Not harming others, and enjoying yourself, are obviously good ideas but are inadequate as a way to think about living a life. As Paul said to the Galatians, self indulgence, without spirituality, leads to dreadful conduct.[4]

The sceptic about Christianity may dismiss our religion as always about "not" doing things. Admittedly the Churches are often their own worst enemies when the only thing people read about them in the papers or on the internet is opposition to something. Whether it is Sunday ferries, or abortion, or same sex relationships. But there is a lot in our society which is wrong and we should not be afraid to speak out, even although amongst ourselves we will disagree on what merits our criticism.

---

[3] John Stuart Mill's famous essay *On Liberty* may be referred to (e.g. John Stuart Mill, *On Liberty, Utilitarianism and Other Essays,* ed. M. Philp and F. Rosen (2015) pp. 5-54).
[4] Gal. 5:16-21.

The more thoughtful and knowledgeable may start with the ten commandments and say that they are mainly negative - stopping things. Terrible isn't it? Having a religion which restricts what you should do. Actually, of course, few people think that it is right to murder, to commit adultery, to steal, to tell lies and to want to possess your neighbour's house and his wife and his possessions. Any legal code, not just a Judaic code, would have these basic requirements. Indeed modern scholars find traces of these ideas in Hittite and Mesopotamian laws, something which once caused problems because some people claimed that God had invented them.

But what about loving others, including our enemies. Showing compassion. Serving others and not ourselves. Forgiving those who do wrong. Helping the poor, foreigners and the disadvantaged. We have a rich basis for a contented and useful existence. Nor should we ignore all aspects of pleasure. For example, the pleasure which comes from beauty, or music, or games. Adding to our joy is the immense love of God.

But could we not believe most of this without involving God? In one sense we could. You could work out a method of living which avoids unhappiness. But how are you going to do that? You are unlikely to want to re-invent the wheel. You might find it in a religion other than

Christianity, which may or may not, believe in our God. You may explore philosophers such as Plato, Aristotle, and Epicurus. That is one approach which for most people is not an easy one. Yet there is here a clue. The word "philosophy" comes from two Greek words - *philos* and *sophos*, meaning love of wisdom. In our society studying wisdom is not fashionable. How much better life would be if our politicians were elected on the basis of wisdom. And wisdom is different from learning.[5] Examinations in schools and universities measure learning, but not wisdom. If we assessed our youngsters on the basis of wisdom the world would be turned upside down.

More likely you go to a bookshop and buy one of thousands of self- help books which promise to transform your life. Although be wary about whether the methods work or work long term. Usually the author has written the book to make money. Occasionally authors write because no one will talk to them. When the National Lottery was first introduced books appeared on the shelves telling us all how to win millions on the lottery. This was as stupid as saying to everyone who plays a lottery or prize draw - "good luck." And the Latin for happy - *felix* - also means lucky. The relationship between good luck and happiness is confusingly built into language.

---

[5] Michel de Montaigne's essay *On Schoolmasters' Learning* (1580) available in several editions is a classic text.

Happiness is not merely working out the correct relationship to material things or to pleasure. It involves dealing with problems which beset us such as addiction, a failed relationship, having no money, or being in poor health, or being injured in a road traffic accident or being lonely or dealing with death. The list is endless. There are answers, to some extent, to all these issues and more in the Bible, although we will never know the true cause of all suffering. The Bible has to be properly understood, and not always taken literally, but in a very sophisticated way it does contain steps for a fulfilling life. The Sermon on the Mount in Matthew Chapters 5, 6 and 7 would be a starting point, along with a good commentary.

Or take Psalm 119. In that one Psalm we can read about dealing with those who are insolent and who scorn you, those who plot against you. Those who persecute you. About avoiding selfish gain and vanity. About humility. About the false values of thousands of gold and silver pieces. About dealing with trouble and anguish. About lies. About how the word of the Lord gives understanding. About the love of the Lord. We tend not to read all its 176 verses in Church, if at any time, so we can miss all this.

Anyone who, in the words of the last verse, is "astray like a lost sheep" could find much to ponder here, although they would have to get past the repetitive phrases that are not in the modern style. It is not a text for the beginner. Psalm 119 then has to be read in the context of the rest of the Bible. And the language of thousands of years ago can require explanation.

The approach of some to happiness is about feelings. A concentration on one's own feelings is where people can go down the wrong path. And in our electronic age there is an emphasis on the "I". On social media and radio and television people talk of how they are feeling millions of times a day. This "cult of the I" is potentially one of the most destructive in our society. It even invades pulpits. There are preachers who fill their sermons with stories of what they have been doing.[6]

Occasionally this is necessary to introduce a topic. But when the preacher is preaching him or herself, not the Gospel, that Church will not be filled with the Holy Spirit, however popular the message.[7]

---

[6] What Professor Cranfield criticised as "those who have self-centerdly and idolatrously insisted on proclaiming their own personal experience as the chief burden of their sermons": C. E. B. Cranfield, *If God Be For Us* (1985) p.147.

[7] Paul stated: "For we do not proclaim ourselves; we proclaim Jesus Christ as Lord ..." 2 Cor.4:5. The idolatory of Christian ministers is also criticised in Matthew S Harmon, *Philippians* (2015) p.128 citing Marcus Bockmeuhl, *The Epistle to the Philippians* (1998) p.80.

Of course, feelings can be important as any counsellor will tell us, and bad feelings can have terrible consequences. Some of us will have scars in our hearts because of the results of depression. But for long term contentment there has to be a solid framework of how our life fits into the scheme of things. It is noticeable that when there is great tragedy, such as the death of a young person, even the most agnostic can leave cards and messages referring to the person being in a "better place" or "playing with the angels" and the like. Many of us search for meaning in this troubled existence.

If you do not have any spirituality in your life you are ignoring the deepest values. You are ignoring the possibility that there is something greater than yourself. Spirituality can take many forms but in essence there is an awareness of a force beyond ourselves, without which happiness is impossible. In Christian terms spirituality means being moved by the Holy Spirit and acknowledging the existence of God. From this it follows that the word of God, as revealed in Scripture, is the guiding force in a happy existence. People who break God's rules damage themselves.

Take, as an example, Paul's injunctions on that most intimate of human activities - our sexual relationships with others. When he was writing to the Corinthians he had to set out how they should behave. The context was a city which was famous for its Temple surrounded by 1000 prostitutes. A society where the wealthy young boys routinely had older male lovers before embarking on relationships with women. A society where slaves could be abused. He had to tell the Corinthians how to behave, and the mere fact that he had to do that indicates that that was different from what they were actually doing.[8]

But there is a problem. If we try to tell young people full of hormones to follow Paul they may ask why they should pay attention to anything said in a very different society in the Middle East two thousand years ago? It is a pertinent question and the answer that it is in the Bible will not impress. More than that, such a response may lead to rejection of the whole Bible.

Texts have to be explained both by reference to the circumstances in which they were written - that is, the problems faced by Paul - and the reasons behind the rules. The aims and objectives of the rules are very important because they can be eternal in a way that the detail required for particular circumstances is not.[9] The reason that Paul wanted to introduce standards, which were even more strict than permitted Jewish

---

[8] e.g. 1 Cor. 5:1 and 9-11; see also Rom. 1: 26-32.
[9] Another example is the many dietary laws in the Bible which are irrelevant for Christians .But the idea that we should thank the Lord, and think of his blessings, and say grace, when we eat, is worthwhile.

behaviour, was his concern for the stability of the society. If there is incest, adultery and promiscuity on a wide spread scale that society will be in trouble. Some individuals, usually women and children, will be badly treated. The extent of fun or pleasure cannot be the only way to judge an activity. Also as Paul wrote to the Romans: "Do not model your behaviour on the contemporary world."[10] Echoed, probably unconsciously, by a famous 19th century philosopher, John Stuart Mill, when he referred to the need for protection "against the tyranny of the prevailing opinion and feeling."[11]

Psalm 1 wants us to meditate on the Lord's teaching day and night, not only on the Sabbath. We should all read a little of the Bible every day. And there are many religious or devotional books which also can be a great help. They can take us to the bigger picture beyond our own existence. In the end the happy person exudes a calmness. An ability to deal with the inevitable problems of life with a serenity. A delight in the beauties of the world around us. A tranquil taking of each day as it comes. The happy person has a body of knowledge to draw on. For Christians also the marvellous realisation that there is a God with immense love for us. We are here in this life, a period of training, with all its sufferings, but for a

---

[10] Rom. 12:2. (New Jerusalem Bible).
[11] *Op. cit.* at p.8.

16

short time, before we pass into the bosom of Jesus. With the hope that when we meet He says to us: "You are my beloved child with whom I am well pleased."

2. Humility

John 13:2-17.

In our text from John there is an obvious message about serving others. Jesus has washed the disciples' feet and he says the disciples should wash each other's feet. It is interesting that John is careful to record precise details of what happened so that the hearers of his message can picture the scene.

Jesus rose from the table, it says. Tables are mentioned frequently in the Bible but translations vary a lot on whether Jesus sat at a table or reclined. The Persian practice, which some Jews adopted, was to recline. This explains Luke's version of the story of the woman who bathed the feet of Jesus with tears, dried them with her hair, kissed them and anointed them with ointment.[12] Luke says that she stood behind him at his feet. This makes sense if he was lying down on his side.

Probably at Passover the disciples would have been reclining on couches on their left sides with their feet stuck out behind them. Leonardo da Vinci in his painting of the Last Supper got it wrong as did Ford Madox Brown in the picture on our

---

[12] Luke 7:36-50.

Order of Service.[13] Jesus rose from the meal. The Good News Bible, and many others, says that he took off his outer garment and tied a towel round his waist. Actually the Greek says he took off his clothes, in the plural, but most translations say it was only his outer robe. The Greek for outer robe was not what John wrote.

There has been a controversy about this for a long time. The first English Bible translation of the New Testament from the Greek manuscripts was by William Tyndale published in 1526. He said that Jesus laid aside his upper garment. But in the more familiar translation of the King James Bible published in 1611, which normally largely followed Tyndale, there was a change. The translators said that Jesus "laid aside his garments; and took a towel and girded himself". The New English Bible of the 1970's referred to "garments' but when the text was revised in the Revised English Bible the word was changed to "outer garment".

Professor Willie Barclay in his translation of the New Testament says that before Jesus washed the disciples' feet he "stripped off his clothes". This is an accurate translation of the Greek. Jesus was really debasing himself and also washing the dirty feet during a meal, his meal, and not before it. You may be a cynic, but what John actually wrote may

---

[13] Ford Madox Brown, *Jesus Washing Peter's Feet* (1852-56).

have been a problem for those Churches which on Maundy Thursday have a ceremony of washing the feet. If the priest, minister or bishop were truly to follow Jesus in front of the congregation there would be an obvious issue. So it is that Bible translations can produce the result that some people think should be there and make a story more palatable and less shocking. In the process there is a distortion of the words of Scripture and a dilution of part of the message.

The picture on the Order of Service ran into this issue. When it was painted by the 19th century English painter Ford Madox Brown it originally depicted Jesus only semi-clad. In the original sketch, which we have, Jesus was naked apart from a towel around his waist which he was also using to dry Peter's feet. This accurate representation of the King James translation caused an outcry when the subsequent painting was first exhibited. The painting remained unsold for several years until Ford Madox Brown reworked the figure in robes in the version we now see in the picture held by the Tate Gallery. Although Manchester Art Gallery has his water colour with Jesus clad only in a towel. The other controversy was his depiction of the disciples as ordinary people which, according to the Victorians, they cannot have been.

Jesus tying of a towel around himself was to show that he was acting like a servant or slave would and also to preserve modesty. Then he put water into a basin and washed and dried the feet. It is a practice well recorded in the Old Testament but usually it would have been done by a servant or slave or by the travellers themselves.

At one level it is an obvious message that no-one is too high to undertake menial tasks, like washing the dishes, or cleaning the floor or putting out the rubbish. We can all do the necessary things to help others, whoever we are. Pride or vanity or status should not stop us.

In John's version of the Gospel, just prior to our text, Mary had anointed Jesus with perfume. In case anyone thought that meant he was the greatest, the one to be honoured, he then goes in the other direction. Jesus accepted an honour, as we should, but subsequently he shows true humility, not the false humility of those who say they are not good enough to receive.

Jesus mentioned humility many times. For example, in the parable of the guests at a wedding feast we are told not to sit in the place of honour, which is a self imposed rank, but at the lowest place, and we may be asked to move up higher. "For all who exalt themselves will be humbled, and those who humble themselves will be exalted." But we can move up higher, if asked. In one of the stories about the disciples Jesus called a child and said; "Whoever becomes humble like this child is the greatest in the kingdom of heaven."

There can be no doubt that humility is vital to being a Christian and we have not even touched the teachings on the subject in the letters of Paul or letters attributed to him. Or the Old Testament such as Psalm 25 where it is said that the Lord leads the humble in what is right, and teaches the humble his way. With a hint that only the humble are following God and have a reward in heaven.

But now the difficult bit. What is meant by "humility"? It is much misunderstood. One of the Greek words for humility used in the NT is more expressive than the English. It is a long word: *tapeinophrosyne*. Greek likes merging words. There are two words.[14] A word meaning low to the ground and a word meaning mind. So it is not being humble in appearance. Or lowly in the sense of riding on a donkey or, in modern terms, driving a cheap car. Or not wearing expensive jewellery or watches. Being humble can be viewed in these ways; a philosophy of the Quakers. Not showing off. But here we are concerned with what's going on inside your head.

---

[14] *tapeinos* and *phren.*

The word "humility" relates to "humus" which means the ground or the earth.[15] This gives us another clue. Humility really means being rooted in the earth. Accurately knowing your good points and bad points. Having an understanding of your talents and abilities and also of your weaknesses. Not being vain but also not downgrading yourself. A true sense of reality. We can be humble and have very strong views. It is not about being diffident. Humility is not the same as being meek. As being someone whom others can trample on. That is the mistake people often make. John the Baptist was humble but he could strongly criticise others. He was not frightened to speak out and eventually it led to his head being cut off.

We can go in the wrong direction. The person who is unduly humble or falsely humble, or who has low self esteem, has big problems. As Aristotle recognised a long time ago, the unduly humble person does not seem to know themselves. They also rob themselves of what they deserve and retreat from doing what they could in life. Low self esteem is a great problem in our competitive society.

On the other hand some of the disciples were not happy with who they were. There are

---

[15] The word "humility" came from the Latin *humus* or "ground" and *humilis* or "lowly" through Old French to Middle English.

several references to a dispute as to who amongst them was the greatest. How many in our society are like that? How many strive to be something else? How many, particularly amongst our young, suffer mental illness as a result? Being truly humble is difficult because we have to assess ourselves correctly.

There are benefits in humility - of knowing your place in the scheme of things. One is that you are better able to help other people. A consequence of humility, perhaps surprisingly, is service to others. In C S Lewis's phrase: "Humility is not thinking less of yourself, but thinking of yourself less." The humble person does not need to concentrate on their own needs. Jesus was constantly saying that he and we should be here to serve. Why we should metaphorically be washing the feet of others and washing the feet of Jesus, with expensive ointment.

Humility is not about having a low status in life. How can it be when Jesus was humble which is a constant theme in Paul's Letter to the Philippians. You can be humble and lead a nation in difficult times. The prime example was Moses. Numbers 12:3 records; "Now the man Moses was very humble, more so than anyone else on the face of the earth." And as the Bible shows he had a fierce resolve especially when all around were doubting his leadership.[16] That illustrates another aspect of humility. It produces a confidence and a belief that you are on the right path. This was recognised by the ancient Roman philosopher Seneca when writing about tranquillity of mind. Humble persons are tranquil. They have a peace of mind because they know themselves. If you are constantly anxious or worried, the chances are that you need to try harder to be humble. To appreciate yourself.

Humility does involve confidence. A quiet confidence. Not thinking you are always right, which causes many problems especially within and between Churches. But more a confidence like Gandhi. If I had to choose one person outside the Bible as a model of humility it would be Gandhi. Sir Richard Attenborough's film *Ghandi* should be compulsory viewing for Christians. Ghandi was not a man with scientific or mathematical gifts or a wish to rule or to dominate others. In his early years as a lawyer, his original profession, he was naive, shy, nervous and soft spoken. The practice of law changed him. Then this modest man, with strong beliefs, transformed lives, and paid for that with his own.

Ghandi was strongly attracted to Christianity. When studying for the Bar in England he read the New Testament and he particularly admired the

---

[16] Ex. Chs. 16 &17.

Sermon on the Mount. The reason he did not become a Christian was because he found that so many Christians were not like Christ. If he did say that, which has been doubted, he may have placed the bar too high. We are not asked to imitate Jesus. That would be impossible. How many crippled people, deaf or blind people have you healed recently just by touching them? For how long have you been without sin? How many disciples do you have? What we are asked to do is different. It is to follow Jesus. The Bible does not ask us to copy its heroes. For example, it would be a nonsense to imitate John the Baptist by dressing in animal skins and trying to live in an uninhabited part of Scotland on a diet of insects and honey. But we can learn from and follow his teaching.

When Jesus stripped off all his clothes and washed the disciples' feet, that was an act of a person who was secure in himself. He was not worried that his position as a Rabbi and Lord would be affected. Truly humble people are strong. They are assured and positive.

Even if you had no Christian belief you could learn a lot from thinking about the Bible and the wisdom of the ages. Sadly in our secular society it is often only religious people who ponder deeply about the right way to live their lives. Reminding ourselves of how we should think and behave is by itself one of the best reasons for studying the Bible and coming to Church.

3. Compassion and second chances

John 8:1-11

The story of the woman caught in adultery is one of the most famous in the New Testament. Some of its phrases have entered into common use in the English language. In the words of the King James Bible: "Let he who is without sin among you, let him first cast a stone." and "go, and sin no more".

And yet it is also in many ways a puzzling story. Is it genuine? It is, for example, in brackets in many Bibles with a footnote questioning its origins. There is also a lot we are not told. What happened to the man who slept with the woman? What did Jesus write or draw on the ground? He did this twice. Why? The woman was not asked if she was guilty of the charge made against her or if she repented. Do we really understand what is meant by "adultery"? It may not be what we think. So it is not all straightforward even if it does contain a beautiful message.

The background is that is generally accepted that the law of Moses in Deuteronomy[17] and Leviticus prescribed death for adultery and, although the texts are not precise, the method of

---

[17] Deut. 22: 22-24; Lev. 20:10. See also Num. 5:11-31.

execution was usually stoning.[18] This seems horrendous to us but it is in the context of standards of sexual morality demanded at the time by Jewish law. These laws were, however, very different from our own. The Talmud[19] records, for example, safeguards to prevent a man even becoming excited by a woman. He was not allowed to gossip with a woman, and especially not with his neighbour's wife. He must never walk behind a woman, even his own wife.

One saying was "A man should walk behind a lion rather than behind a woman."[20] This would mean that most men in this congregation have already sinned several times this morning, in this Church. According to the ancient Jewish rules if a man walked behind a woman who was crossing a stream, that is a woman above running water, he was forever barred from the world to come. The point for present purposes is how easy it was to commit a sexual sin, but also how complicated, and to us strange, the rules were.

We cannot be sure how the rules were applied in practice at the time of Jesus but it is possible that the strictest rules were only followed

---

[18] Ezek. 16:38-40.

[19] Of course, we have the problem that the date of the Talmud is later than the Gospels. But it (and the Mishnah) are amongst the best indications we have of the old Jewish rules.

[20] Abraham Cohen, *Everyman's Talmud* (2008) p.104.

by Pharisees who usually operated in an urban setting. They hint at one reason as to why impractical it might have been for Jesus to have chosen a woman as one of his 12 disciples.[21] It could be that his otherwise close relationships with women were unprecedented in Jewish society, but that is a topic for another sermon or three.[22]

So far as adultery was concerned the Jewish law was different according to whether you were a man or a woman. A married man was allowed to have an affair with an unmarried woman. That was not adultery. A married woman committed adultery if she had an affair with any man. Provided they kept away from married women,[23] married men were free to roam. A married woman was not.

So, for example, the married Abraham could have an intimate relationship with the slave Hagar.[24] King Solomon, who had many wives, also had three hundred concubines.[25] Probably for wealthy married men sleeping with female slaves

---

[21] A more important reason was the failure to educate girls so they could be disqualified from preaching and healing which were to be important functions of the disciples; Hayyim Schauss, *The Lifetime of a Jew* (1950) p.97.

[22] J.E. Stambaugh and D.L. Balch, *The New Testament in its Social* Environment (1986) p.104; Schauss, sup cit., p.126.

[23] Deut. 22:22.

[24] Gen. 16:1-4.

[25] 1 Kings 11:3.

was commonplace. It certainly was not prohibited by the Jewish view of the laws of God. In modern parlance, mistresses were allowed provided they were not married. When King David slept with Bathsheba that *was* adultery because she was married to Uriah the Hittite.[26] And David then arranged for Uriah's death in battle. David and Bethsheba's adulterous and murderous relationship produced Solomon listed by Matthew as one of the ancestors of Jesus.[27]

One reason for the distinction between married men and married women was that a married woman was the husband's possession, which must not be defiled. It is distasteful to us but a husband or his family paid money to her father to get her and so she belonged to him.[28] The prohibition on adultery in the ten commandments is often misunderstood. It was about a wife being property. The Jewish practice was similar to rules in other societies at the time. The effect of these rules was also an attempt to be sure of the paternity of a child. To avoid the comment, in the American phrase, "Mama's baby; papa's maybe."

In any event, what the NT does not tell us, is that the Jews ran into difficulty with a harsh law on adultery which was discriminatory between the

---

[26] 2 Sam.11:2-5.
[27] Matt.1:6.
[28] Jack R. Lundbom, *Deuteronomy* (2013) p.635.

sexes and had a severe penalty, death, to be applied without discretion or mitigation according to the circumstances. It became ridiculous to punish a woman and not a man and when adultery became widespread Rabbi Johanan ben Zakkai suspended the laws on adultery just prior to the destruction of the Temple in 70 AD.[29]

When Paul was writing to the Corinthians and to the Romans he had a problem when discussing how people should live their lives. The Jewish rules on permitted sexual behaviour were unsatisfactory, as we have seen. The practices in the Greek and Roman worlds, where Paul was preaching, were very lax even by modern standards. Corinth was famous in part because of a Temple with one thousand prostitutes around it and there was much more about that society, including relationships between young and older men, which Paul, the Pharisee, would have found repugnant.[30] The result was that Paul in his letters to the Corinthians and to the Romans invented a system of sexual ethics which has dominated Christian teaching ever since.[31] It made the Christian Church very different from other groups in that society. It promoted and protected the

---

[29] Jacob Milgrom, *The JPS Torah Commentary, Numbers,* (1992) p.348.
[30] A. N. Wilson, *Paul:The Mind of the Apostle* (1997) pp.161-163.
[31] James D. G. Dunn, *The Theology of Paul the Apostle* (2003) pp.689-692

position of women and slaves and introduced for all some measure of equality which was revolutionary. But we are here concerned with the Jewish rules which applied at the earlier time of Jesus. The Jewish rules which Jesus would have known. It is reasonable to assume that he recognised that they had issues.

There is debate about the extent to which the death penalty for adultery was actually enforced in practice and, at some stage, under Roman rule, the Jewish authorities lost the right to impose it. So the Pharisees who found that a married woman had committed adultery had a problem as to what to do about it. They came to Jesus with the woman, calling him Rabbi or Teacher, apparently as it were to seek legal advice. They were setting a trap for Jesus. Was he going to say - "ignore the law of Moses" - or was he going to demand that the Roman law be ignored. Should she be stoned or not? A simple "Yes or No" answer, Rabbi. Also if he said that her sins were forgiven, he would be claiming to be God, which was blasphemy in their law. Whatever the answer they thought that he would make powerful enemies. They wanted to accuse him. Their motivation had little to do with adultery.

But to Jesus there would have been another problem. In their nastiness they were humiliating a woman in the Temple, a very public place. They brought the woman to him while he had people around him whom he was teaching. The Pharisees seem to have interrupted. It would have been one thing to seek his opinion in private or to attend his early morning class and ask a question or two. But they paraded the object of their hate. Some have speculated that the woman might have been a bit disheveled but we do not know. We can guess that she was terrified. What would you feel if you were facing a death sentence which could be quickly implemented. They made her stand before everyone. This is what happened to Peter and John before the Council.[32] It was the position for judicial examination. But the Pharisees' motivation was different from an inquiry into the woman's conduct. They already seemed to have satisfied themselves as to what happened. They wished to trap Jesus. They were using the woman as a thing, for their own purposes.

No matter how annoyed he was, Jesus took his time. We might not write or draw on the ground - we have paper or iPads - but pausing in silence, and doodling, are valuable practices when we are faced with a difficult question. His answer that only those without sin could cast the first stone was brilliant. Not least in the context of the Jewish law which any Pharisee would say that they strictly observed. Sins included any feeling of sexual attraction towards the woman, hypocrisy, listening to gossip, hatred, or even walking behind her. They

---

[32] Acts 4:7.

probably realised that the feelings in their hearts and their actions, with a disregard for the humanity and dignity of the woman, could also mean that they had sinned. And sin was in their theology a rebellion against God.

Jesus had a message for the Pharisees which they may not have appreciated. It is also relevant to us. We should look at ourselves in a mirror, in a harsh light without make up. In particular, religious leaders, including elders and preachers, should not claim to be holier than thou.[33]

The Pharisees left, with the elders leading the way. What Jesus then did is remarkable. He did not condemn the woman for a breach of the ten commandments, but he did not let her off either. He did not say never sin in *any* way again, which would have been an impossibility. In the context, what he did tell her to do was to stop her affair.

We do not know her circumstances. What drove her to seek the arms of another. What the attitude of her husband was. Whether there were children. What the long term offered. To end the affair might have been very good advice, regardless of religious laws. Even in the context of those laws he was giving her a second chance. It

---

[33] A phrase which comes from Isa. 65:5 in the King James Bible.

was as if he was imposing a suspended sentence. He showed compassion to her, which the Pharisees did not.

There is here another lesson for us which is unrelated to the complicated Jewish concepts of permitted sexual conduct. It shows how a Christian should react to someone who has misbehaved. The Pharisees were concerned about her past and penalising her for it. Jesus was talking of her present and her future. He was showing pity. He wanted her to reform. The Pharisees wanted to condemn her.

Most of us of any age have made a mess of something in our lives. None of us would always get 10 out of 10. Jesus does not blame us for the mistakes we have made but provides us with hope for the future. He gave the woman a second chance - but he did want her to change. It was not a simple matter of sins are forgiven. There was a "don't do it again" message. We would like to know what happened next but we are not told. The final judgment would only come, as with us, when her life ended.

The text is not in several early manuscripts of the Gospels and there has been much debate as to who wrote it and whether it is genuine. The details are not our present concern but the majority view is that it is a story about Jesus, which is why it is in modern Bibles. It may have caused problems for the early Christian Church because they interpreted it as condoning adultery, but a later view prevailed that that is not the true meaning. It is about second chances. It is about how we should treat others and how we would wish to be treated ourselves when we make mistakes.

God is eager to save us. He is a God full of mercy, kindness and compassion. For those who sin but seek him he is keeping them safe. In the words of Julian of Norwich "It is true that sin is the cause of all this suffering, but all shall be well, and all shall be well, and all manner of things shall be well…"[34]

---

[34] The quotation will be found in Julian of Norwich, *Revelations of Divine Love*, (sometimes called *Showing of Love*) The Long Text para 27, and in essence in other sections, available in numerous translations. She was an English anchoress and Christian mystic and theologian (c.1342-c.1416).

4. Secrecy and compassion

Mark 1:40-45 & 7:31-37

Why did Jesus "sternly warn" the man with a skin disease. Indeed the Greek used for "sternly" is unusual and suggests anger. Jesus said, with great emotion, "Listen, don't tell anyone about this". Why when he cured the deaf man with a speech impediment did he order the people not to speak of it to anyone? But the more he ordered them not to, the more they spoke.

These are not the only two instances of the secrecy of Jesus. When he healed the blind man at Bethsaida he sent him home telling him not to go into the village.[35] Like a judge imposing some sort of ancient bail condition. When he healed the daughter of Jairus he put the crowd outside and, after raising the child, strictly ordered the parents to tell no one.[36]

Many other passages show the reluctance of Jesus to heal.[37] For example: "And he sighed deeply in his spirit and said, "Why does this generation ask for a sign? Truly I tell you, no sign will be given to this generation."[38] A rather angry

---

[35] Mark 8:26.
[36] Mark 5:43.
[37] e.g. Mark 9:14-29: Mark 8:12; Luke 11:29; Matt. 12:39.
[38] Mark 8:12.

Jesus. He was not willing at first to do anything in response to his mother's statement that the wine had run out at the wedding in Cana. In that case some bible translations temper what Jesus actually said. In the NRSV Jesus said to his mother, "Woman, what concern is that to you and to me? My hour has not yet come."[39] A son annoyed with his mother. Yes, even Jesus. Nor was Jesus inclined to show off to demonstrate his power. Famously in the temptation of the devil he did not turn stones into bread or throw himself off the highest point of the Temple.[40]

We are here concerned with the secrecy of Jesus' miracles. There seems a paradox. The ministry of Jesus was public but he did not want everyone to know what he had done to help people. A very different approach from many modern politicians.

He would have anticipated that crowds seeking a miracle would interfere with his life. After healing the man with a skin disease he could no longer go into town openly but stayed out in the country.[41] When he healed two men with demons which went into a herd of pigs Jesus got into trouble as everyone from the town came out and

---

[39] John 2:4.
[40] Matt. 4:1-11.
[41] Mark 1:43-45; Matt.8:4.

told him to leave this non-Jewish territory.[42]   Not surprising as the owner of the pig might have been well known in the community. He was deprived of his herd without compensation, although what might have happened was that the pigs became alarmed by the shrieking of the men with demons. Not that Jesus destroyed the herd.

So why did he heal at all when it caused him problems? This is when it gets really interesting. In the first reading today the Good News Bible says "Jesus was filled with pity, and stretched out his hand and touched him'".[43]   But, commendably, a note to the passage makes clear that some manuscripts say that Jesus was filled with anger.[44] Are you filled with anger when you see someone with a serious, life changing, illness? How can we explain that emotion? As Rowan Williams puts it Jesus had "anger at the way in which illness imprisons people."[45]

In the context of healing the word which may be translated as "anger" really reflects a visceral sense of compassion for the afflicted. Anger which is just can be a spur to action. The catalyst for

---

[42] Mark 5:17; Matt.8:34.

[43] Mark 1:41.

[44] A similar note is in the NRSV while the Revised English Bible uses the word "anger". The issue is authoritatively discussed in Bruce M. Metzger, *A Textual Commentary on the Greek New Testament* (2nd.ed. 1994) p.65.

[45] Rowan Williams, *Meeting God in Mark* (2014) p.34.

tackling injustice throughout the centuries, for example: abolishing slavery, the absence of votes for women, racial discrimination, or the abuse of children by clergy. So anger can be linked to compassion for victims. Those watching Jesus were not sure which emotion was dominating his thinking. He probably had both. He was a very emotional person.

As it is said in our first passage, "Jesus was filled with pity." But he wanted to act in private. Remember in our second reading about healing the deaf man it is written: "So Jesus took him off alone, away from the crowd." Of course treating someone in private can be a respect for their dignity. But there may be an indication that if we are going to do good we should preferably not broadcast the fact. We help others to help them: not to increase our own prestige.

If you change water into wine at a wedding you cannot do that in secret, which was a reason for not doing it at all. Although at first the steward and the bridegroom did not know that Jesus had been responsible. Mark is careful to record that. There was no attempt by Jesus to show off or broadcast his powers or to seek a vote of thanks. He would not have wanted that. He came to glorify God, to whom the praise was due, not himself. Sometimes we should do the same.

Some distinguished scholars think the reason for secrecy was that he did not wish to draw the attention of the Roman authorities. This is not convincing. The society was full of magicians and false prophets and healers and another one was no threat to Roman occupiers. The Romans, generally, allowed their conquered nations to keep their own religion, but they and the Greeks had their own beliefs about healing. They had shrines for the god of healing -Aesculapius in the Latin, - a son of Apollo. They worshipped that minor god, whose rod and serpent have been used as a symbol by, amongst many others, the British Medical Association and the Royal Army Medical Corps. This pagan symbol of faith healing, and a false god, is still with us, used by respected institutions.

Taking all his miracles together the dominant theme is that Jesus was so moved with strong compassion at terrible long term suffering, or even the problem of disgrace at a wedding, that he could not help himself. Even if it meant being run out of town. He had to heal. Even if it disrupted his life so he had to avoid people and go to lonely places. We should help others even if it costs us.

Indeed compassion was so central to his nature that there are many examples of him not following the strict Jewish code on, for example, healing on the Sabbath, or touching and talking to a person with a skin disease. He didn't follow all the laws despite one contradictory insertion in Matthew who was trying to convert a Jewish audience.[46] What he did was warn against religious zeal when it gets in the way of compassion. His teaching and his actions were an attack on fundamentalism, which Christian people have tragically often ignored.

That is the real truth behind the parable of the Good Samaritan.[47] Two people "passed by on the other side", a phrase from the King James Bible known to many who never come to church. One was a priest and the other was a Levite, who was a lay assistant who helped in the Temple, especially with music. Both would not want to chance the possibility of being involved in ritual defilement by touching a dead body. They were concentrating on their own holiness. The Samaritan had no such religious scruples. He ignored the possible application of rules in the Torah.[48] He bound up wounds and took care of the injured traveller, at his own expense. He gave the innkeeper some money in advance - enough according to some calculations for 24 days board - and in effect he gave the innkeeper a blank cheque by saying "when I come back I will repay you whatever more you spend." A rather dangerous invitation to an innkeeper. He took risks. Someone

---

[46] Matt. 5:17.
[47] Luke 10:25-37.
[48] Lev. 21 and Num. 5 &19.

who was stripped, beaten and half dead, possibly unconscious at the roadside, would not be cured in a few days, especially when the only medicines used on the wounds were wine and oil. Also the Jewish text, the Mishnah, shows that public innkeepers had a very bad reputation.

The Samaritan "was moved with pity" or, again, in the King James version "he had compassion on him." Indeed both translations, and things do get lost in translation, fail to reflect the more urgent Greek which is *esplanchnisthe* a word related to other words meaning a feeling by the Samaritan as strong as a movement of the bowels.[49] An interesting use of language especially when two of the other characters were much concerned with purity laws and keeping clean.

It can be an interesting question as to what we would do if faced with the same situation as the Samaritan. We might try first aid and call the emergency services and leave them to deal with the issue. Pass the problem on. But note that the Samaritan, in Jesus's words, did more than first aid. He spent money and promised to pay future sums. He said he would come back to visit the beaten man, a stranger. He showed real compassion by several actions.

---

[49] Strange as it may seem to us the bowels were thought to be the seat of love and pity. We prefer to think of the heart.

The Gospels give us vital principles which should govern our lives. Sometimes we will succeed: sometimes we will fail. Jesus was providing us with clues as to how we should think and act. We often have to try to work out the details, but most of us are given brains by God to do this. No teacher, not even Jesus, can give the student the answer to everything.

The Gospels do not give us a code of what to say or to do, for example, when faced with someone in distress at a diagnosis of cancer or someone whose relationship has broken up and who can talk of nothing else, or on seeing the man sitting in the high street doorway with a piece of cardboard saying he is hungry and homeless when he may be neither. They do not provide an answer to all the questions of how to deal with migrants or refugees. Or even how to cope with someone who misbehaves, such as another motorist who cuts us up: although, in that event, we may want to avoid an explosion of the bowels.

But, if we are to follow Jesus, we must adopt the principle of compassion. It is an aspect of love for our neighbour, the central theme of the Gospel message. And the feeling should be very strong. However clumsy or inaccurate language may be at expressing it. It should be deep. Compassion should govern our lives even if it costs us. Even if it costs us an uncertain sum.

Remember the shortest sentence in some of our Bibles in the English language. "Jesus wept".[50] You will know that was the reaction to seeing Mary weeping because her brother Lazarus had died. Jesus shared, he felt, her grief, her loss. Maybe some of his own as well, because he probably knew Lazarus. The Greek also suggests that he had anger in his mind.

I use the word compassion rather than "pity". Language is important and difficult when describing emotions. But "pity" in current usage can be used for just feeling sorry for someone or even with some slight feeling of contempt or disregard or criticism. "It's a pity that .." "What a pity it is raining today". "What a pity we cannot play golf." "What a pity he is preaching today." "Compassion" means in its Latin origins, *com* - together and then unusual Latin for suffering. Sharing suffering. Feeling the other person's pain. Jesus felt Mary's pain and showed it. If the Son of God can weep, so can we.

Of course, there is, as always, a balance. If we gave all our money to the poor, they would have to give it back to us. We should not sacrifice ourselves unnecessarily and cause further problems. Nor use so much energy doing good that we burn-out, which is not helpful for anyone. Even Jesus got tired and needed to escape for a while.

---

[50] John 11:35.

We do not need to do extraordinary things, but ordinary things well and with empathy for others.

Sometimes we can help only a little. One Catholic priest was troubled, as priests often are, by the ringing of the door bell at about 10 pm and a man, smelling of drink, saying that he was hungry. He was always invited in but the priest made sure that the jam sandwich he was offered used the cheapest Mother's Pride bread.

There is, though, an even broader point and another aspect to compassion. If you did show compassion towards every human being, of whatever race or religion, or none, you could not be cruel to them. You would not be able to improve all their lives but you do not harm them either. We should try to feel the pain of others even if we are not sure what pain they really are feeling. The other motorist may have had a bad day at work or an argument with a spouse. We do not know, but we start with gentleness and love towards other human beings. We all have problems.

If the human race adopted an approach of compassion to all human beings, unable to hurt others, there would be an end to war. It is that important. Compassion could mean that what we pray for frequently has occurred. We will be close to God's Kingdom coming on earth as it is in Heaven. And don't keep it secret. You can tell people about it.

5. Serving with a thorn in your flesh

Exodus 4:10-17.
2 Corinthians 12:7-10.

One of the remarkable things about the Bible is the stories of the way in which God used people who had disabilities which might have led them to think that they could not serve. Take Moses. He had committed murder when he thought no one was watching and he hid the body in the sand.[51] But this was found out and he had to flee for his life. When God later pleaded with this refugee from justice, again and again, to lead the Israelites out of Egypt, Moses argued that he would not be listened to or believed. And as a last throw in his argument: "O my Lord, I have never been eloquent, neither in the past nor even now that you have spoken to your servant; but I am slow of speech and slow of tongue." Eventually he said to God: "please send someone else." How often have we said that when we have been asked to do something we did not want to do. God got angry or impatient and eventually Moses agreed. But remarkably it is revealed that there was a more fluent speaker available, his brother Aaron.

Now if there had been a modern job application and an examination of CVs Moses would not have been selected. A speaker who was

---

[51] Ex. 2:11-15.

not good at speaking, he may have had a stammer, and who had a controversial past. Against someone three years older and an eloquent spokesman. Aaron was also an ordained priest, a Levite. God did not act like a human appointing committee. He probably never does.

Mary, the mother of Jesus, was probably an illiterate teenager in a tiny country village who was asked to carry out an incomprehensible task. To bear a child to be called Jesus and more than that, the angel said, - the Son of God. Mary would have been of lowly birth, living in basic accommodation, and dressed much more crudely than artists over the centuries have suggested. No blue or red dye, which were luxuries, or fine gowns. More likely homespun in a brown colour which would have concealed the stains of village life.

And, of course, God chose someone who was not married to bear the child. Whatever your view of the virgin birth, there was going to be a scandal in that society, which was a good reason, amongst others, for leaving town and going to relatives in Bethlehem. Even the Koran, which surprisingly has many sentences about Mary, tells of Mary and the birth of Jesus. It records her retiring to a far off place but says there was childbirth under a palm tree which is not our belief. And Mary's response to an incredible request? According to Luke, if we are to take his narration as historically correct, it was: "Here am I, the servant of the Lord, let it be with me according to your word."[52] What if she had said "No!"?

We come forward in time to Paul. What an incredible choice to do God's work. One of the most zealous persecutors of Christians in the country. He approved of the killing of Stephen. He ravaged the Church and entered house after house and dragged off both men and women to prison. Some of them died. He was as bad as any member of the Gestapo. I was talking to a Danish person who in 1944 in Denmark remembers her mother answering a loud knock at the door. Opening it with a babe in her arms and two toddlers clutching her skirt, there was a German soldier. He had the wrong address. The neighbours were shot. The fear of one of those children transmitted to me earlier this year over coffee. Paul was that soldier.

He even went abroad to Damascus, with the express intention of finding and bringing people back to Jerusalem for punishment. In his own words he had zeal as a persecutor of the Church. He was trying to destroy it, as the Nazis tried to eliminate the Jewish race. Not only did he not have

---

[52] Luke 1:38. The infancy narratives were late additions to Matthew and Luke and there has been extensive doubt as to the extent to which they are historically correct: Joseph A. Fitzmyer, *The Gospel According to Luke (I-IX)* (1981) pp.306-313 and 335. The discrepancy with Matthew where the announcement is to Joseph is but one of the issues.

the CV to be an Apostle he had the opposite. Would Eichmann have been appointed a Rabbi?

But there is more. His letters form a large part of the New Testament, although there is controversy about which ones he actually wrote. He was sophisticated and learned, and he has to be judged by the literary standards and methods of his day. You will have your own view about whether he was a good written communicator.[53]

One of the books which did not make it into the New Testament describes Paul. The *Acts of Paul and Thecla* say that he was short, bald and had bowed legs. His eyebrows met and he had a rather large nose. In 2 Corinthians 10 Paul himself mentions a criticism made of him: "his bodily presence is weak, and his speech is contemptible".[54] He also admitted in 2 Corinthians 11 that he was no speaker.[55] This itinerant working craftsman, this wee bald man with bandy legs, who was not a good speaker, was chosen by God to broadcast the Good News.

But Paul also had a thorn in his flesh. The Good News Bible translates it as "painful physical

---

[53] It has been suggested that clichés from rhetoric show that Paul must have had a modest education: Gerd Theiseen, *The New Testament* (trans. John Bowden) 2003, p.66.
[54] v.10.
[55] v.6.

ailment" but that is a very free translation of the one Greek word *skolops* - meaning a thorn or, perhaps, a stake - as in a pole with a sharp end. Most Bibles refer to "thorn". Indeed the phrase "thorn in the flesh" was first introduced into the English language by the King James Bible.[56] It, and its common variation "thorn in the side", are classic phrases of the English language. There has been much debate as to what illness this refers to. There have been arguments from demons to bad eyesight caused by Paul's Damascus vision. We are in that advanced realm of history known as speculation. One modern hypothesis is that it was malaria. In the place of his birth, Tarsus, there was the climate and geography, with swamps, which would have encouraged mosquitoes to breed. Tarsus had a reputation for malaria and Alexander the Great when he entered the town was infected by malaria which disabled him for two months. It might be what killed him 10 years later, or lowered his resistance to another disease, but we do not know.

Paul's illness was sporadic and produced great pain. Like a stake driving deep into him, which reflects the headaches which malaria can sometimes give. The condition affected his ministry. As he said to the Galatians: "it was because of a physical infirmity that I first

---

[56] Tyndale in 1526 referred to "unquietness of the flesh" which does not have the same ring.

announced the gospel to you; though my condition put you to the test, you did not scorn or despise me, but welcomed me as an angel of God, as Christ Jesus".[57] Ancient Galatia was in the Highlands of modern Turkey and the cooler air may have been beneficial for a fever.

Although much ink has been spilled for millennia on the meaning of "thorn" it may be helpful that Paul's handicap is not specified. So we can relate to him with our bad back or painful hip or poor eyes or our depression or migraines; whatever our thorn is that limits what we can do. Three times he prayed to the Lord to have his condition removed. That was natural. His prayer was unanswered in the sense that what he wanted was not given to him. But God did reply, perhaps after the third prayer, that His grace was sufficient. 2 Corinthians 12 v. 9 says: "My grace is sufficient for you, for power is made perfect in weakness."

We may be called on to do tasks for which we do not feel suited because of our personal history, perhaps of misdeeds, or our perceived lack of skill, or a long term ailment. The message of the Bible is that that may not be a good reason for refusal. Was God wrong when he chose Moses, Mary and Paul? Look at what they did. Also in each case He called on them to do something very difficult.

---

[57] Gal.4:13-14.

We may not be asked to do momentous things but simple and basic things. Jesus was served by having his feet washed or being anointed with perfume.[58] Jesus was also given a meal by Martha.[59] Someone had to cook his meals and clean up afterwards. God and his Church need people who do the outrageous and difficult things and also those who make the tea and the coffee. Christians are called on to act as well as to believe. We need deeds more than we need creeds. And as it is said in the Letter to the Colossians[60]: "whatever you do, in word or deed, do everything in the name of the Lord Jesus, giving thanks to God the Father through him."

If you were giving a present to God, would you rummage through your old second hand clothes or unwanted Christmas gifts, or even look in your dustbin? No. You would buy the best you could afford: - the most expensive perfume, for example. So it should be with all service. That is the underlying message of the last book in the Old Testament, Malachi. At that time one service to God took the form of offerings in the Temple. The priests were offering the lame and sick and blemished animals. The Lord said: "Cursed be the cheat who has a male in the flock and vows to give it, and yet sacrifices to the Lord what is

---

[58] Mark 14:3-9; Matt. 26:6-13; Luke 7:36-50; John 12:1-8.
[59] John 12:2.
[60] Col. 3:17.

blemished."[61] So we must always do our best with what we have when we serve the Lord in this Church and elsewhere. Second best is not what God wants, but he accepts that we may not be the greatest.

Paul was told by God that he had fitness enough to do the tasks for which he had been chosen. He could have done more if his body had been fitter and his communication abilities greater. The weakness was there to make Paul humble and, maybe also, enable him better to identify with those who were suffering. Something as a young man he definitely did not do. God's grace was sufficient. God's power was enough.

Worse than giving God second best is not giving at all. As Jesus said "For the Son of Man came not to be served but to serve ..."[62] We are meant to be servants. The word Jesus used is, in the Greek, *diakonos*, from which we get "deacon". But Jesus was not thinking about a particular rank in the Church. The word *diakonos* can equally be translated as "minister". In one sense all Christians are ministers or priests or ambassadors of Christ[63], here to do God's work. We are not meant to think only of our own salvation or to be a spectator at a church service. It is selfish to concentrate on our

---

[61] Mal. 1:14.
[62] Mark 10:45; Matt.20:28.
[63] e.g. 2 Cor. 5:20.

own holiness. We are to do God's work with God. We need to remember that next time God asks us to do something. We are all human and there will be times when, like Moses, we keep saying "No!" We may even believe that someone else is better qualified. But it is never too late to say "Yes!"

There are also occasions when God wants us but people reject us. One of the most famous and successful 20th century preachers was George Campbell Morgan. He had no formal theological training. When he applied to be a candidate for the ministry the Methodist Church rejected him. They said he was an incompetent preacher![64] His father sent him a telegram: "Rejected on earth; accepted in heaven." And so it proved to be.

Young Morgan was eventually ordained by the Congregationalists. His preaching became so famous that in all he crossed the Atlantic to preach in Canada and the United States 54 times, some feat in the early part of the 20th century. Often not a well man, with throat problems and headaches, not ideal for a public speaker. As a child he was so sickly he could not go to school and had to be privately taught. He published 71 books of sermons and bible study. He worked hard. He used his talents. His lack of formal training in

---

[64] Warren W. Wiersbe, *50 People Every Christian Should Know* (2009) p.274.

theology he turned to advantage by his own careful study of the bible. He brought thousands to Christ and shepherded a Westminster Church through parts of two world wars. He died in 1945 at the age of 81.

When we serve, in whatever way and with whatever knowledge and talents we have, even though we are not the best, God will help us and our reward will be great. Those who serve the Almighty are blessed and remembered.[65] As Jesus said in John 12[66]: "Whoever serves me, the Father will honour." Which means God reveres or treats as precious. Yes, those who respond to God's call by serving in the community and in this Church, in whatever way, great or small, are valued by God as precious. Blessings on you all.

---

[65] Heb. 6:10.
[66] v.26.

6. Worry

Matthew 6:24-34

The punch line in the passage read from Matthew is what most people remember. "So do not worry about tomorrow, for tomorrow will bring worries of its own. Today's trouble is enough for today." There is the oddity that, as you may have noticed, the thrust of the whole passage is actually also on worrying about today. Three basics are mentioned - food, drink and clothes. In the early morning if you are poor and starving, or thirsty, or have inadequate clothes for the weather, you very well might be anxious about what happens later in the day. The ordinary people who Jesus was addressing depended on the day's income from work. They would have had few savings and there were limited charitable payments. The inability of the breadwinner to work on any day because of illness, or accident or loss of a job, could mean that they and their family starved. They were extraordinarily vulnerable. They had reason to worry. They needed to pray for their daily bread. Perhaps that is why Luke in his version of the story omits this punch line about tomorrow.

My main concern is the impression you may have that Jesus is saying "Do not worry, God will provide." Jesus did not say this. He was not saying that you should be feckless and not try to have a job or an income, or not insure your house, or not take safety precautions such as wearing a helmet when cycling. The problem is the translation which gives us the word "worry" and the inadequacies of the English language to have words for degrees of worry.

The word 'worry" comes to us from Old English which means "to strangle" or to try to tear apart as in dogs worrying sheep, a phrase we still use. But at some point the word "worry" was extended for dramatic effect, so that instead of just being anxious we are always worrying, - about when the plane will depart, or if we will get a parking ticket or if the grass will be cut or if the cake was in the oven for the right time. Jesus was not talking about that type of worry. The Greek is *merimnoa*. This is a combination of two words. It means "pulled apart" or figuratively "to go to pieces." About tearing ourselves apart. Toxic worry that can affect our health.

Jesus's audience were mainly Jews and they would have understood because the Rabbinic philosophy was that life should be a combination of prudent management of our affairs plus serenity about the future. We should arrange things so that we take care, but the future, today or tomorrow, is unknown and we should not worry about it. We should not worry about the future because we have trust in God.

Anxiety can be beneficial. If your car breaks down or your child is ill or you lose your job, or you have a diagnosis of serious illness, anxiety can lead you to take steps to deal with the problems. Jesus was talking about what has not happened - the "What if?" worries. What if the car does break down, or what if the child falls off the bicycle, or what if the lump is malignant? Tearing yourself apart about something which might never occur. Jesus was telling us to have faith in God who loves us, without limits.

Faith is not just about belief. That is only the first stage. You can believe that there is a spiritual being which created the Universe, called God. You can believe all that is said about the life of Jesus, including his resurrection. But to have faith in a person, let alone God, requires not only that you recognise their existence, but that you trust them. The very word "faith" derives ultimately from the Latin *fides* whose primary meaning is "trust".

Faith is not shown by the routine of attending Church on Sunday and going to every communion service as an insurance policy, especially as we get older. God will go beyond the formalities, and look at whether we really trusted him and his love for us. Faith is not just belief or doing good works. Faith is belief combined with trust.

But faith need not appear to be exuberant. You do not need to be a great evangelist and wave your arms in Church at the mention of Christ. Faith can be the size of a mustard seed, said Jesus.[67] A seed which can grow. Paul tells us in Romans 10 v.17 that faith comes from what is heard about the word of God. *That* is a good reason for coming to Church. And for listening to the sermon, which sadly sometimes may make you feel that suffering is a part of Christianity. That verse in Romans had a great effect on the famous American preacher Dwight L Moody who concluded: "Church attendance is as vital to a disciple as a transfusion of rich, healthy blood to a sick man."[68]

When you see Jesus he may not ask you "Did you believe in God?" but a different question. "Did you have trust in God?' And after your answer a follow up: "Then why did you spend sleepless nights tossing and turning and worrying about something which might never happen?" We all have to think how we would reply. Professor Willie Barclay wrote that worry and failing to trust God was a sin.[69]

As Martin Luther said, "Pray and let God worry." And he knew about anxiety. It is discussed

---

[67] Luke 17:6.

[68] Read more at
http://www.brainyquote.com/quotes/quotes/d/dwightlmo3865
98.html

[69] William Barclay, *The Gospel of Matthew* (3rd ed. 2001) vol.1 p. 301 states: "There may be greater sins than worry, but very certainly there is no more disabling sin."

in Erik Erikson's book on *Young Man Luther*. At one time Luther developed a severe anxiety, protracted and bordering on melancholy. Mind you, he had just married. He was a monk and she was a former nun. A year later Luther entered a prolonged and serious period of depression.[70] The psychiatrist Erikson thinks Luther had an endogenous psychosis.[71] This has been disputed[72] but there is no doubt that he was often chronically ill. You can be a great Christian though you have mental illness, an anxiety disorder. John Knox also suffered from depression and a strange, obsessive, personality.[73] But they both prayed. And they transformed peoples' lives.

As it is put in the First Letter of Peter[74] addressed to a Christian church under serious stress. "Cast all your anxiety on him[75] because he cares for you." Or Paul while in prison, perhaps facing execution, in his letter to the Philippians "Rejoice in the Lord always; again I will say, Rejoice! ... Do not worry about anything, but in

---

[70] Erik H Erikson, Young Man Luther (1959) pp. 235-43.

[71] *op. cit.* p.231.

[72] John Wilkinson, *The Medical History of the Reformers* (2001) pp 16-18.

[73] There are many references, sadly not indexed, in Jane Dawson, *John Knox*, (2015). These episodes are said to be transient by the physician Wilkinson, *op. cit.* p. 101, without a detailed analysis, but opinions may differ.

[74] 1 Pet. 5.7.

[75] i.e God.

everything by prayer and supplication with thanksgiving let your requests be made known to God."[76] Faith can be weak, but re-appear, especially when you face disaster or death. I once heard an army commander say that there are few atheists before battle.

The difficult philosophy of Jesus as to how we should live our lives, is reflected in many disciplines which seek to remove stress. Meditation, mindfulness, yoga, pilates and the like. Concentrate on the present, on the now. And if we do not become stressed about the uncertain future, we might actually do what worry cannot achieve. We might be healthier and happier. We might live a bit longer.[77]

Of course, we all worry too much and we will fail to follow Jesus's words from time to time. None of us is perfect. Even the disciples - in the presence of Jesus. Remember the story given to us by Mark[78] and Matthew[79] of Jesus asleep in the stern of a boat when a storm arose and threatened to sink the vessel. After a woken Jesus had calmed the wind and the sea he said to his disciples: "Why are you afraid? Have you still no faith?" *No* faith! But Jesus still loved them. We need to ponder that

---

[76] Phil.4:4 & 6.

[77] A book which some have found helpful is Will van der Hart & Rob Waller, *The Worry Book* (2011).

[78] Mark 4:38.

[79] Matt 8:24.

story when a tsunami hits our lives, literally or metaphorically.

So what happened to the lilies in the field? They are not mentioned in some translations and yet they are one of the most memorable images of the teaching of Jesus to those of us brought up using other translations such as the King James version of the Bible: "Consider the lilies of the field, how they grow, they toil not, neither do they spin: and yet I say unto you, That even Solomon in all his glory was not arrayed like one of these."

It is a translation problem again. Those of you who are gardeners might have wondered how there could have been fields of wild lilies in the soil and climate of Palestine. Your wonder would have been justified. There may have been about 3000 species of wild flowers, we cannot be sure, but only one lily, and it was probably uncommon. With the anachronistic precision of the modern botanist it was *lilium candidum* or the Madonna lily, which today grows mainly in the mountains. Some think the reference in the Bible was to poppies or anemones, but the safest bet is to think of wild flowers in general, like the annuals you may sow

The mention of them is more than a colourful image. It also contains a metaphor, a story within the story. It is deliberately recorded that the grass is here today and gone tomorrow, burnt up in the oven. The grass was thrown into the oven which was a large hole in the ground with clay sides, rather like a tandoori oven, and the thin bread baked on those sides. In a country with few trees, wood was precious. One form of fuel was dried grass. In their recent book on St Kilda, Angela Gannon and George Geddes record that one of the fuels used by the inhabitants was turf,[80] presumably complete with any wild flowers.

We are here but a short time and our lives may end prematurely, and suddenly, as Jesus's did, like the flowers burnt before they had naturally faded.[81] But while here their brightness, their colour and the enjoyment they give, is a symbol of how we should be viewed by others. Think of that the next time, and every time, you look at flowers. We should have a carefree simplicity in our lives like birds, flowers, or little children. And we should pray.

The Christian life includes a prudent management of our affairs with a serenity about the future. In Lina Sandells' words which we sang, and which have been treasured throughout the world for two centuries, live life day by day. And as Psalm 118 says. "This is the day that the Lord has made: let us rejoice and be glad in it."[82]

---

[80] Angela Gannon and George Geddes, *St Kilda: The Last and Outmost Isle* (2015) pp 89.113,
[81] Foreshadowed in Isa. 40:6-8. "All people are grass."; "surely the people are grass".
[82] v. 24.

Love your enemies

Leviticus 19:17-18 & 33-34
Matthew 5:43-48

I asked for the passage from The Old Testament passage from Leviticus to be read from the New Revised Standard Version of the Bible because some translations distort the words so that the passage does not offend Jews. But that also spoils the contrast Jesus was trying to make.

In the reading of the first passage we heard that there is an apparent element of racism. You must not hate people of your own kin, that is of your own tribe or clan. As a Jew you must not hate Jews. But what of those of a different race? You can make up your own mind on the meaning. It is not surprising if the passage has been interpreted as saying you must love your neighbour and hate your enemy. Jesus mentions this version. And then contradicts it.

But Christians, in their criticism of Judaism, have sometimes ignored our second passage, Leviticus 19:33 to 34, which commands us to love the alien including the alien who resides with us - a very relevant comment for today. There is here a classic illustration of the dangers of taking one verse of the Bible without reading the whole passage.[83] Separating related thoughts by 15 verses may not be clever drafting but we are dealing with a text written over a long period with numerous additions and editing possibly some 3,500 years ago. At a time when Scotland was in the Bronze Age.

We heard from Matthew 5. But in Matthew 22 Jesus mentions the command to love your neighbour as yourself[84]; again a separation of texts. I am concentrating on the more difficult command in Matthew 5 to love our enemies. Jesus is trying to make us love all without limits. Just as God does not send sun or rain only onto the fields of the righteous. But on the fields of the wicked also. His love is impartial.

Who are our enemies? We all have them. The word "enemy" comes from the Latin *in amicus* that is, not a friend. Someone who is unfriendly or hostile. It would be difficult to avoid such a person somewhere if we travel or shop or work. And in our personal lives it is notorious that there can be an apparent absence of love somewhere in families and in clubs or organisations including, sadly, within Churches, and between Churches, where there are not always beacons of light and love. When I hear it said of a good person that he or she

---

[83] See the point being hinted at in Frank Crusemann, *The Torah* (1996), p.5.
[84] Matt. 22:39.

had never had an enemy in the world, I wonder if they had any contact with human beings. We are deluded if we think that everyone is our friend.

Jesus does not tell us to love our enemies in the same way as we love those close to us, our children, our friends, our family or our spouse. As is well known Greek had at least four words for love, all with different meanings: *agápe, éros, philía*, and *storgē*.[85] Only *agape* and *philia* occur in the New Testament.[86] Here we are dealing with *agape* love, which we cannot translate into English with one word. *Agape* does mean that we do good to others and show them goodwill. It is the love of God for his children. We have to love our enemies as God loves us. That is a very tall order. Jesus's yoke may be easy and his burden light but this is difficult.

Actions are better than too much cerebral thinking about the meaning of *agape*. The hateful or spiteful neighbour or family member or ex spouse or partner or work colleague may seek to harm us and upset us. We could hit back and try to hurt them. We could say bad things about them. We will dislike them even more and they us. If we smile, take them a present, treat them with dignity,

---

[85] There was also *ludus, pragma,* and *philautia*.

[86] A traditional sharp division between the two terms has been criticised as "nonsense" on the grounds that there is an overlap: Paul Foster, *Colossians* (2016) pp. 139-140.

look for the good in them, we have the potential to transform the situation for the better. Maybe not always succeeding, but it is the right way forward. *Agape* love seeks nothing in return unlike other forms of love. Jesus was trying to teach us what love really is. As Martin Luther King said: "Love is the only force capable of transforming an enemy into a friend."

Does that mean that in more extreme circumstances you must be a pacifist. Some of us will remember the sixth commandment in the King James Bible: "thou shalt not kill". But in modern translations it is now: "Do not murder", which is different. Murder is intentional killing without legal justification. Most Quakers, but not all, are pacifists. But so far as I can gather their attitude to killing is complex and varied. As one Quaker said to me she would do whatever was necessary to protect her children, even if it meant using the kitchen knife to kill an intruder. As she put it: "I would die for my faith: but I would kill for my children."

Martin Luther King gave a powerful sermon on our very passage in Matthew in Montgomery, Alabama in 1957. The text is now easily available on the internet. He preached non-violence as the way forward for ending racial inequality. But take this scenario, which is very different from the context in which Martin Luther King was speaking. You are a policeman in Paris with a terrorist in the sights of your rifle. The terrorist is about to shoot innocent people in a cafe. Do you pull the trigger, or say "I must love this person and not kill him"? I assume that if you were a believer in non-violence you would not be that policeman. But what is the Christian justification for ending the life of the terrorist?

If you are a parent I hope that you love your children. I also trust that you have not allowed your children to do whatever they wanted. You have sometimes said, stop doing that. You have imposed discipline. But you continue to love them, even when they have been bad. You can love the person but not love the deed. You can try to stop the deed if it will do harm.

Christians do not need to be people who are gentle saints who would never harm a fly - although we must respect those who take that approach. We live in a world full of pain. We are beside those who deliberately try to make our lives a misery and we are not far away from serious crime including terrorism. So we need police, prisons, and armed forces[87] but also Geneva Conventions on how we treat the enemy in war and also conventions and rules on human rights on

---

[87] See also Paul in Rom.13: 4 who was dealing with us being subject to the State, what he called "the authority". He said: "But if you do what is wrong, you should be afraid, for the authority does not bear the sword in vain!"

how we treat fellow citizens, even those in prison. In the words of Dietrich Bonhoeffer, who had first hand experience of living with the Nazis who eventually executed him. "We can say "No" to sin and "Yes" to the sinner".

You can puzzle over why at the conclusion of the Last Supper, Jesus told his disciples to sell their cloaks and buy swords; a passage maybe often skipped over, or treated as metaphoric, by preachers.[88] It is intriguing to read Bible commentaries on this passage as some theologians worry as to whether Luke's text is a mistake. It does not correspond with their idea of a loving Jesus. But Jesus was practical just as Christians are realists. Jesus believed in defence, but two swords were enough. And a sword was, of course, used, in the Garden to cut off an ear of a slave. Jesus then healed the slave, his last healing prior to the Cross.

Another passage which causes trouble is when Jesus used violence. He cleared the money changers from the Temple. The account is, unusually, in all four Gospels, so we must take it seriously, but in John[89] it is at its most dramatic, probably because John was an eye witness. (Dramatic, that is - provided you do not read a translation which sanitising things so that people

---

[88] Luke 22:36.
[89] John 2:13-22.

are not upset or a common view of Jesus challenged).

First, Jesus made a whip out of cord. Using his whip he drove out the money changers, and the sellers of the animals, and the sheep and the cattle. He was obviously very angry. He scattered the coins and then overturned the tables left behind. He was a bit gentler with the sellers of the doves but he gave them verbal abuse.

An angry Jesus on the rampage with a whip, committing what in modern Scotland would be a good breach of the peace and assault. Maybe also possession of an offensive weapon. Did he hate the money changers and the sellers of the animals? No, but he hated their actions and took steps to end them. Steps which he must have known would have a serious effect on him. His actions did not please the Temple authorities, and what he did hastened his trial and crucifixion.

Jesus loved and forgave those who disagreed with him and those who persecuted him. What a shock Judas must have had when he approached Jesus in the Garden, followed by Roman soldiers, to betray Jesus with a kiss. Jesus knew what was going to happen. He greeted Judas with the word "Friend".[90] Do we say that to someone who has tried to upset or undermine us?

---

[90] Matt. 26:50.

Let alone someone seeking our capture and maybe our death?

Some manuscripts of Luke record that while on the cross Jesus said: "Father forgive them, for they do not know what they are doing."[91] When Stephen was being stoned he knelt down and cried out in a loud voice: "Lord, do not hold this sin against them."[92] He was showing *agape* love to his executioners.

In this country during the reformation that great man George Wishart was condemned to death, partly blown up by gun powder, then hung and burnt at the stake in St Andrews on the orders of Cardinal Beaton. It is reported that Wishart kissed his executioner on the cheek and forgave him. This was on 1st March 1546. In May of that year a group of Protestants invaded the Castle at St Andrews and murdered Cardinal Beaton. They had mixed motives for killing Beaton, with a careful plan, but they claimed, according to John Knox, that they had been sent by God to revenge Wishart's death. They paid no attention to Deuteronomy 32.v. 35 where it is said it is for the Lord to avenge; a text quoted by Paul in Romans 12 v 19. Tit for tat killings are forbidden by Paul who says we must not repay evil with evil.[93]

---

[91] Luke 23:34.
[92] Acts 7:60.
[93] v.17: see also 1 Pet. 3:9.

If after 9/11 it had been said by those in power that we must try to understand and to forgive, how different the world now might be. But there is a fundamental difference between Christians and politicians, not that a politician cannot be a Christian - that would be absurd. Christians do not seek votes or popular approval. Jesus was very unpopular in his time. The disciples were also disliked. In Jesus's words in John 17 "the world has hated them".[94] It is a paradoxical and uncomfortable truth that those who love are not everywhere admired. Look at what happened to Jesus and Martin Luther King. Or what is happening now to Christians around the world in at least 60 countries. Each month over 300 Christians are killed because of their faith. The number may be much higher. Some may die today.

Nearer to home the history of Northern Ireland shows the devastation and misery caused by revenge killings. A strong person can break the chain and then there is a way forward. The weak person seeks retaliation. This was recognised thousands of years ago in Proverbs and later repeated by Paul.[95] Proverbs 25:21 says: "If your enemies are hungry, give them bread to eat; and if they are thirsty, give them water to drink; for you will heap coals of fire on their heads." In other words it frustrates the enemy by denying them a

---

[94] v.14.
[95] Rom. 12:20; see also Ex. 23:4-5.

pretext for another attack. And the coals of fire are a symbol for the burning pain which results. This is in a text which possibly pre-dates Levlticus. Composed, even if not written down, when Scotland was in the Stone Age. It was Nelson Mandela's insight that "If you want to make peace with your enemy, you have to work with your enemy, then he becomes your partner."

The hateful person - the other person on the committee, the neighbour or ex spouse or ex partner, or the family member or the work colleague or the terrorist - wants us to retaliate because they are comfortable in creating a world of distress and fear. That is what they understand and it makes them feel superior. It is not the world God wants. In the face of love without limits fear does not prosper.

Mathew and Luke in their passages about loving our enemies[96] say we should pray for those who persecute or abuse us. Prayer is a good start. And the First Letter of Peter tells us that even if we do suffer from doing what is right, we are blessed.[97]

While we must prevent evil happening, and sometimes there are great evils like Hitler who must be stopped, we should be on guard that we

---

[96] Matt. 5:44: Luke 6:27-36; see also 1 Pet. 3.9.
[97] 1 Pet. 3:14.

do not add to the evil in this world. It is a difficult message not only because retaliation is a natural feeling but because Churches in the past have not been free from this sin. For example, Cardinal Beaton who unjustly tried and executed George Wishart. Protestants who in revenge killed Beaton and helped to lay the foundations of the Church of Scotland.

If the message of the Bible could be heard, understood and followed it would save our chaotic and dangerous world. The teaching of Jesus is leading us to establish God's Kingdom both in our personal lives and throughout the earth. A kingdom where, in the metaphoric imagery of Isaiah, the strong and powerful co-exist with the weak and vulnerable, "The wolf shall live with the lamb, the leopard shall lie down with the kid; the calf, and the lion and the fatling together, and a little child shall lead them."[98]

---

[98] Isa. 11:6.

8. Breaking down Barriers

Jeremiah 22:1-9
Galatians 3:23-29

We all have a social identity. You may be a Scottish woman, a Christian, and a supporter of Nairn County Football Club. This may mean, by definition, that you are not a Frenchman, a Muslim or a fan of Paris St Germain. However we list the many factors which make up our identity, including our sexuality, we are all part of several clans or tribes. And other people are different.

When we examine the history of the human race we find that almost all wars are wars between those of different tribes or groups. Whether it is clans fighting in Scotland or Eskimo or Australian aboriginal villages frequently attacking neighbours. Or wars between nations in Europe. Or the present troubles in the Middle East. At another level it can be football supporters who shout abuse at, and assault, those who wear a different shirt or scarf.

A case could be made that the most serious problems in our world have always been caused by our identity. An identity which leads to a dislike or hatred of, or by, others who are different or foreign. The phenomenon of the tribe or clan has been at the root of terrible evil and grief. Humans are not alone in this behaviour. It has also been found amongst chimpanzees in the 1970's study in the

Gombe Reserve in Tanzania. Even ants can recognise and attack ants which come from another group.

Of course, Christians are not like that are they? We do not discriminate between Jews and Greeks, between males and females.[99] Really? Christians love their enemies because the Bible tells them to. But in the First World War the Germans prayed for victory as did the British, both supported by their pastors.[100] Nor is the Bible the most obvious source of texts about peace amongst nations or tribes. When the Israelites were wandering in the wilderness they sought safe passage through the land of King Sihon of Heshbon. When this was denied they fought and as Deuteronomy 2:34 records: "we captured all his towns, and in each town we utterly destroyed men, women and children. We left not a single survivor." Sounds like genocide committed by God's people. They repeated this in the land of King Og[101] and in the conquest of Canaan.[102] The Holy Land was founded on bloodshed and massacre.[103]

---

[99] As well as our text in Galatians see Col. 3:11.
[100] The idea that God can be on our side in fighting enemies can be derived from Deut. 20:4, but this was in ancient times.
[101] Deut. 3:6.
[102] Josh. 11:21.
[103] See also the rules of warfare in Deut. 20: 12-14 about putting all males to the sword when a town resists and that "You may take as your booty the women, the children, livestock, and everything

Those who attack our religion, or don't believe in it, can challenge us with these passages. How is it possible to worship with a book which records what would now be called war crimes done in God's name at his command? Is that our God? Should God be put on trial as the Rabbis, for other reasons, did in Auschwitz?

All of us may have to answer these questions especially if someone challenges us as to why we go to Church. There are several possible approaches. The first is to point out that God in fact allows us to follow our sinful ways. He does not intervene to stop us. Nor may God approve even when we claim it was in His name. We should also look for God's message in the whole Bible not in isolated passages written by fallible human beings in very different circumstances from ours.[104] Christians have not always done this with horrible results. At one time the Church of Scotland persecuted witches because Exodus 22:18 says: "Thou shalt not suffer a witch to live." Around 4,500 unfortunate women died in Scotland as a result, often after torture. Mental illness and just being different or eccentric were regarded as sins by ministers and kirk

---

else in the town, all its spoil. You may enjoy the spoil of your enemies, which the Lord your God has given you."

[104] The approach adopted to interpretation of the Bible is similar to that in C E B Cranfield, *The Bible and Christian Life* (1985) pp. 6-11.

sessions with terrible consequences. This cannot have been the will of God.

In South Africa the Dutch Reformed Church supported apartheid. It also established three separate churches one for blacks, one for coloured or racially mixed persons and one for Indians. Its theology was based on texts such as the story of the Tower of Babel in Genesis 11, the speaking of different languages in Acts 2 and passages in the book of Revelation. Views changed in 1986 but difficulties remain in practice.

The history of the Jewish race in the Bible can be seen as embodying racism and worse. Psalm 137 starts with a line made famous by Boney M. "By the rivers of Babylon". But the last verse of the psalm is not in the song. It is "Happy shall they be who take your little ones and dash them against the rock!" Approval for killing babies part of our religious texts? Yes. But we have to look carefully at the circumstances behind the words.

Taking just Exodus, although there is much dispute there may be nearly one thousand years between, on the one hand, the Israelites' exodus from Egypt and the occupation of Canaan and, on the other hand, the writing of the texts which describe the events that took place. By the time of the book of Exodus there was a less militaristic attitude. The book combines thoughts from very different eras. There are bits of history but also some elements of later morality. For example, there are passages telling us to act with love for enemies.[105]

Views changed. Views can change in religion. We no longer follow the practice of male circumcision, although it is in God's covenant with Abraham of all places. Our attitudes to slavery have altered. In some Churches women can now speak, even preach, despite two passages prohibiting this.[106] Nor in this Church do women routinely wear hats or veils although a traditional view was that this was required by Scripture.[107] There may even be, dare I say this, wives who do not obey their husbands, despite obedience being required in three places in the New Testament.[108] Current debate is about Paul's references to homosexuality.

Sometimes views must change as we gain a better understanding of the texts, including the circumstances in which they were written. It is why it can be important to refer to the Jewish practices and thinking at the time the texts were written. In the past people misread the Bible because they did not do this. The Archbishop of Canterbury, Justin

---

[105] Ex. 23:4-5 and 9; see also Lev. 19:33-24.
[106] 1 Cor. 14:34; 1 Tim. 2:12.
[107] 1 Cor. 11: 5-16.
[108] Eph. 5:22-24; Col. 3:18; 1 Pet. 3:1.

Welby, put it very well last year. He said that the Church must speak "with the humility of a reformed alcoholic who recognises that they once practised the very things they now urge people not to do."

In the beautiful story of Ruth's life in our Bible she and her mother Naomi showed in Hebrew - *hesed* i.e. fidelity and commitment. A valuable lesson. The relevance to the present sermon is that the heroine of the story, Ruth, was not a Jew. Ruth was a foreigner from Moab. Deuteronomy 23:3 to 6 excludes Moabites from the Assembly of the Lord because of ancient hostility. But Ruth is named as one of the ancestors of Jesus.[109] Inter marriage with a foreigner is built into the family tree of Jesus.

By the time of Jesus there was a further shift in thought. Jesus, while his main mission was to the Jews, showed kindness to strangers: from the Syrophoenician woman to a Roman centurion.[110] And he would talk to a Samaritan woman at a well. Matthew 25 v.35 and again v. 38 says that we are blessed by God if we welcome a stranger. I will not elaborate on what happens to us if we do not do this. We can all read in verse 46 about our eternal punishment.

---

[109] Matt. 1:5.
[110] Matt. 8:5-13; Luke 7:1-10.

Amongst Jesus's last instructions to the disciples when he appeared to them after the resurrection was that repentance and forgiveness of sins was to be proclaimed in His name "to all nations."[111] Nearly his last words in Scripture! - "to all nations". After all, one view of DNA analysis, based on research published in Nature in 1987, is that we are all descended from mitochondrial Eve who lived about 160,000 years ago in East Africa. We may all be related. Some people do not like that idea. Racists hate it.

As this country searches for a new identity in Europe,[112] and the world, we have to be wary about a retreat into a narrow concept of who we are and how we relate to others. There is xenophobia in our society. One Greek word we have all heard. As you know it means an unreasonable fear, distrust, or hatred of strangers, foreigners, or anything perceived as foreign or different. It would be too easy for our society to move in that direction. The post Brexit hate mail, easily traced on the internet, is terrifying. Foreigners are described as vermin and worse.

But we need more than pious repetition of phrases such as loving neighbours. Or concepts such as tolerance with which many would agree.

---

[111] Matt. 28:19; Luke 24:47; Mark 16:15.
[112] The referendum vote to leave the European Union was on 23 June 2016 and at the time of the sermon was creating much uncertainty and some xenophobia.

For example, as the Bishop of London has pointed out, it is sometimes said that a problem with immigrants is that they do not even learn our language, or they mainly speak their own. But this works both ways. As well as helping them with English, the natives of this land could attempt to learn some of their language and their culture. The cry that "They do not integrate" is not the response of a Christian.

We are meant to welcome strangers, and why should integration be in one direction only? For example, are sufficient steps taken by us to welcome those in our area with nationalities or religions different from most of us? Particularly at this difficult time. Some of them will be very worried about their future.

We should, at least, make people from elsewhere feel welcome in our midst, by meeting them and offering them a meal or a snack. It need not be anything grand. A cup of tea and a smile can go a long way. Nor should we be parochial and ignore what other Churches do with success.

Romans 12:13 tells us to extend hospitality to strangers, not just to think about it or to say "It is a good idea but ..." And Paul in Romans was not only talking about people of the same faith. In the words of Pam Pettit's hymn which we sang[113]: "for

---

[113] "I have a dream" a man once said, v.4.

thoughts and words don't ease the pain: unless there's action, all is vain; faith proves itself in deeds."

Of course, we are not naive and we might be rejected. Other people can distrust us and our motives. Barriers can work in both directions. But did Jesus give up because he was rejected? Is perseverance not part of the Christian way? We need to show others that there is common ground and shared objectives. A Church worthy of the name is not just about the personal salvation of its members. Although there is a long history of missionary and charitable work, every Church needs, from time to time, to do a reality check in case it is becoming too much of a club or clique, turning in on its self and existing mainly for the benefit of its congregation.[114] The Christian message is about reaching out to others - to all nations.

The warning in Jeremiah,[115] and elsewhere in the Old Testament, is that if a nation acts without justice and righteousness to foreigners, and to the disadvantaged, and moves away from God, that nation will become a ruin and a desolation. Thomas Cole's painting on our Order of Service[116]

---

[114] C. E. B. Cranfield, *If God Be For Us* (1985) p.22.

[115] A similar passage is Mal. 3:5.

[116] Thomas Cole, *The Course of Empire, Destruction* (1835 -36).

is part of a series of five about the history of an imaginary city from its growth to decadence and then its inevitable fall. In the fourth picture, which we have, there is destruction of the city. In the final picture there is desolation. No human beings. The landscape returning to nature. An image too bleak to put on the Order of Service. Humanity has been destroyed by its own conduct.

In this nation we are all in the same ship. If we make a mess of our journey the ship will hit the rocks and we, or our children's children, will all drown, including those with first class tickets.[117] If Christianity can do any good on the Earth it is by breaking down barriers between human beings of different clans, including those of other religions or none, and not just by talking about it. And we should start close to home.

---

[117] This is an example taken from a sermon by the Bishop of London, Rt. Rev Richard Chartres on 24th Dec. 2015.

9. Judging Others

Luke 7: 36-50

In many stories in the Gospels there are good guys and bad guys. In our text there are only two persons identified, apart from Jesus, but there were obviously others at the table. The first sentence starts with a Pharisee inviting Jesus to dinner. Maybe some of the original hearers of Luke's script booed at this point. Like the tradition of the pantomime the first to enter from stage left is the pantomime villain.[118] Then the good fairy enters stage right. In medieval times hell and heaven were placed on these sides.

But as is typical of the Gospel stories things are not straightforward. The Pharisee appears to be a good guy. He had invited Jesus to dinner. He addresses Jesus as "Teacher" so he may be expected to listen and learn. But there was something strange about this dinner invitation.

When Jesus entered the Pharisee's house he was not given the normal courtesies. A kiss of welcome, water for his dirty feet, and olive oil, used

---

[118] On the other hand amongst Jews the Pharisees may have had a good reputation for their piety: Joachim Jeremias, *Jerusalem in the Time of Jesus* (1969) p.266. Jesus's attacks on the Pharisees would have been unpopular and they led to the cross. Luke, however, was probably writing for a Hellenistic world.

in those days like soap, as a refreshment for his face or head. In our culture we have different customs. Our guests do not normally walk in sandals through hot, dusty, rough and unpaved streets to their destination. But if someone arrives as an invited guest we would probably take their coat, ask them how their journey was, suggest where they might sit and then offer a liquid refreshment. Not doing all that would be very odd. Jesus would have been within his rights to get annoyed. Instead he takes his place at the table, reclining on his side with his dirty feet, which would have been obvious to all present. Probably not sitting at a table as Rubens[119] and other artists thought and some Bibles say. The Greek for reclining on a coach was used. The honoured guest was not being honoured at all. But Jesus did not appear to react. It is, after all, good manners to ignore bad manners.

The good fairy, - the woman who bathed and anointed the feet of Jesus, - she had a murky past. What her past was has been a matter of debate. It was obviously known to the Pharisee. In our text she is described as a sinner and it is said that she had many sins. The Greek word is *amartolos* which does mean sinner or hardened in sin. Its derivation explains what sin is. The word is a metaphor. The

---

[119] Peter Paul Rubens and Anthony van Dyck, *A woman washes Jesus' feet in the house of Simon the Pharisee* (1615).

related verb *amartano* is literally "missing the mark", like an archer, or making a mistake. With the consequence of not sharing in the prize. Of not being awarded the Olympic medal. We are not told what the sins of the woman were. But, remarkably, generations of biblical scholars have not been satisfied with that. They have said that this unnamed woman was a prostitute. This may be true but it is not what the text says.

Mary Magdalene is mentioned in the next passage in Luke. The calumny has been extended to the view that she was a prostitute. But there is no justification whatsoever for saying that she had an immoral past. Nor for identifying her as the same woman who washed Jesus's feet in our text. The link that they were the same woman, who was a prostitute, may first have been made in a sermon in the 6th century by Pope Gregory 1.[120] He was a great Pope but on this point he has read into Luke what is not there or anywhere else. But he was so authoritative that he has been accepted, by Catholics and Protestants, even when he was mistaken. Myths in Christianity have a life of their own and there are many of them and sometimes they are repeated from pulpits.[121]

---

[120] The myth is said to derive from a homily (No xxx111) delivered at the Basilica of St Clemente in Rome on 14th September 591.

[121] There was also the quite different story of Mary anointing the feet of Jesus in the house of Martha and Mary in Bethany told in

Some years ago, before Dan Brown, you might have made your fortune by claiming that Mary Magdalene was the wife of Jesus and that they had children and there is a conspiracy in the Vatican to hide the truth. If only we could have access to the secret files!

It is difficult enough to understand the meaning behind Scripture without preachers inventing what is not there, particularly when the human fascination with sexual matters means that what is said is remembered even if it is wrong. Any court lawyer could defend this woman in our text against unstated and unproven claims; and who knows how much of it was just gossip about a woman who was attractive to men? It is also regrettable that in a male dominated society and a largely, if not entirely, male produced Bible the Pharisee is given a name, Simon, but she is anonymous. Yet the person Jesus related to most in the story was a woman. If Jesus had written a Gospel, and so far as we know he never did, it would be good to think that he would have named her.

The woman was not invited to the dinner, but heard about it. So she comes into the house like a gate-crasher. But not to eat. She bursts with emotion at the sight of Jesus, perhaps in part because of the disgrace of his dirty feet, and she goes to him,

---

John 12:1-8. Confusion around the identity of Marys in the Gospels is commonplace.

behind him, as he would be lying down on his left side. Her tears are so copious that with them she bathes the feet of Jesus.

Then she does something even more remarkable. She dries the feet with her hair, not with the robe she would have been wearing. By now the onlookers would have been truly horrified. To use her hair she would have had to take off any head covering and undo her long hair. That seems to have been the greatest disgrace for a Jewish woman to do in the presence of men. One source says it was grounds for divorce.[122] Loose female hair was thought by the Rabbis at the time to be erotic. But there was also a symbolism which would not have been lost on those who saw or heard about the event, but which is not so obvious to us. In traditional Middle East society a bride on her wedding night lets down her hair and allows her husband see it for the first time.[123] She was making a statement about her relationship to Jesus.

The woman had come with an alabaster jar of ointment. The alabaster box or jar, a soft stone cruse, was the most luxurious of its kind and the ointment would have been perfumed. She brought Jesus a present of expensive smelly stuff. She used it to anoint his feet, more than the Pharisee would

---

[122] Misnah, Ketuboth 7:6.
[123] Kenneth E. Bailey, *Jesus Through Middle Eastern Eyes*, (2008) pp. 248-249.

ever have done, and she kissed his feet many times. The Pharisee, in his thoughts, despaired of this woman touching Jesus. The language in the Greek has a hidden message. The word used for "touch" is a reference to an intimate connection. And all this was taking place in public, in his house at his dinner table!

Everyone would have waited for the reaction of Jesus. They would have expected a Rabbi to be very annoyed and to ask for the outrageous woman to be ejected. Instead he accepts what the woman has done and turns on his host. By now all the onlookers are completely aghast.

The woman must have known who Jesus was. She was showing love, because she realised her sins had been forgiven. We don't know how she knew that but she obviously had deep faith. The text is ambiguous but verse 47 implies that she was showing gratitude for what God had already done for her. Jesus merely confirms that her many sins were forgiven.

One of the issues with Christianity is how difficult it is to behave the way we are meant to. The Sermon on the Mount has some very hard messages. For example, do we never get angry without justification? Do we always love our enemies, that is those who are not our friends? Do we ever fall into the category mentioned in 1 Timothy

5:13 and gad about from house to house as gossips and busybodies, saying what we should not say?

The story of the woman in Simon's house shows that there is a way out of many sins. She repented and was forgiven and her joy was immense. Perhaps everyone in the room, maybe in the village, rejected her but she had something precious. She had the *agape* love of Jesus. If you feel alone in the world and you think that there is no point to life, Jesus is always there for you. He will not reject you. He will give you peace and show you love. Always. We should not beat ourselves up about things we have done wrong in our lives. The love of God and Jesus is so great that there is a way forward. In the words of Julian of Norwich, "though I do nothing but sin, my sin shall not prevent the working of (the Lord's) goodness."[124] But first you have to realise that you need forgiveness, as the woman did: but Simon did not.

There is also another message for us. It would be better to be that woman, that caring, fallible, emotional woman, than to be the Pharisee. We all sin, because we are not perfect. We make mistakes or miss the mark in our relationships with others. We do not always win a medal for the way we behave. But the Good News is that Christ came to save us.

---

[124] Julian of Norwich, *Revelations of Divine Love*, Long Text para. 36.

Luke is doing more than giving us a story of a dinner party with an unexpected twist and a message about forgiveness. He was warning us about being like the Pharisee. All church going people are in danger of becoming the modern equivalent of Pharisees. People who know the rules on how they should live their lives and who think that, by and large, they follow them. The risk then is criticism of others and thinking that we are better. That is what the Pharisee in the story did. He placed himself above the woman in his thoughts.

The Pharisee had not learned the lesson mention by Paul in Philippians. Paul wrote: "Do nothing from selfish ambition or conceit, but in humility regard others as better than yourselves. Let each of you look not to your own interests, but to the interests of others."[125] There is one very interesting short word in the English language which can express disapproval or criticism, used by basic players of Scrabble. It is the word "tut", often repeated: "tut, tut". Said with superiority as a rebuke.

In Luke 6 Jesus said: "Do not judge, and you will not be judged: do not condemn, and you will not be condemned. Forgive, and you will be forgiven; give, and it will be given to you."[126] We have to be wary of our own faults. He went on to say in a famous passage; "Why do you see the speck in your

---

[125] Phil. 2::3-4.
[126] vv.37-38.

neighbour's eye, but do not notice the log in your own eye."[127]

Jesus related better to the woman who had done much wrong in her life, probably hurting a lot of people, but who genuinely repented and sought forgiveness. But also a woman who continued to act contrary to the normal behaviour in her society. That last point is important. Too often our criticism, under our breath, is of someone we see who looks different or behaves in an unusual way.

Of course, acting in strange or eccentric ways may disqualify a person from a certain job, as may their lack of abilities. And sometimes there has to be judging. One classical Greek illustration was of judging a poetry or play contest.[128] We also need people to judge disputes or sentence criminals. But we are talking about judging another human being as a person who is inferior to us or who has less worth. The Father with his enormous love will view that person differently. He made them in his image, male and female.[129] Do not judge and you will not be judged.

---

[127] Luke 6:41.
[128] e.g. Aristotle *Poetics* is a classic text at the origins of literary criticism.
[129] Gen. 1:27.

10. Solitude and silence

Exodus 33:7-11
Mark 1:35-39

I want to take you back to what Nairn was like about 150 years ago.[130] The time of grandparents and great grand parents. There were no radios or wirelesses, or televisions. Nor computers. Nor phones of any type. No planes overhead. No neighbours playing loud music on electronic devices. Apart from the sounds of nature there were few man made intrusions. The carts and coaches on the rough streets and the newly arrived railway. There would have been blacksmiths, carpenters, masons and fishermen. There would have been some commotion from 3,500 people living together in a very small space mostly around two streets. The blast of a horn from an arriving coach seems to have been unwelcome to some.[131] But otherwise the noise of daily life would not have been very different from what it would have been for much of the four thousand or so previous years that humans have inhabited this area. Those who were outside the small burgh would in their rural life have had a daily solitude and stillness which it is now difficult to imagine.

---

[130] This sermon was delivered in Nairn URC Church but the sentiments extend to any Scottish town.
[131] Isobel Rae and John Lawson, *Doctor Grigor of Nairn* (1994) p.69.

Yet it is in an agricultural community, not too dissimilar, that Moses, Elijah, Jesus, John the Baptist and others sometimes sought extra solitude and silence. Which does raise the question as to whether in our spiritual life we need to make more efforts to follow their examples.

There is a long Christian tradition of seeking silence as a way of getting closer to God. The Desert Fathers and the Desert Mothers lived in the Scetis or Nitrian Desert in Egypt from about the fourth century to the seventh century AD. Their withdrawal from society was part of the origins of monasticism and the records of their sayings have had an important effect on Christian thought because of the monks' and nuns' reputation for holiness and wisdom.

For example, "A hermit said, "Take care to be silent. Empty your mind. Attend to your meditation in the fear of God, whether you are resting or at work. If you do this, you will not fear the attacks of the demons." Abba Moses said: 'Sit in your cell and your cell will teach you everything." The most famous Desert Father, Anthony, said: "He who sits alone and is quiet has escaped from three wars: hearing, speaking, seeing: but there is one thing against which he must continually fight: that is, his own heart." Goodness knows what Anthony would have made of smartphones.

It would not be wise for us all to become celibate hermits, but some silence on a regular basis and especially at vital times in our lives can be important. Take Moses in our passage from Exodus.[132] Moses had a very difficult job, which he did not want. The Israelites were constantly rebelling against his leadership. In the verses just prior to our text God described them as a "stiff-necked people." In the previous chapter while Moses was delayed on the mountain receiving the first two tablets of the covenant the Israelites had made and worshipped the golden calf. Moses in his anger broke the first set of tablets and, of course, had to go up the mountain again to get replacements. No doubt to his irritation, to put it mildly. To cope with this indisciplined tribe Moses used to take his tent and pitch it far off and there communicate with God. Not always on his own as his assistant, Joshua, was with him.

When Elijah was fleeing from Jezebel he went into the wilderness under a solitary broom tree.[133] He was suicidal, but help was at hand. An angel spoke to him twice and after a long journey he spent a night in a cave when the Lord also spoke to him. The result was finding Elisha and the renewal of his ministry.

---

[132] Ex. 33: 7-11.
[133] 1 Kings 19:1-18.

When David was fleeing from the irrational Saul and then from his son Absalom he spent a long time in the wilderness.[134] A lot of this was to escape from enemies but one of the most beautiful Psalms, Psalm 63, is said to date from one of these periods. David saw and spoke to God in the wilderness.

Jesus kept going into the wilderness to escape the pressures of his life and when vital decisions had to be made. For example, before choosing his disciples,[135] after feeding the 5000 and before walking on water,[136] to recover from hearing the news about the beheading of John the Baptist[137] and sometimes just to be alone in the dark and to pray prior to a busy time.[138] Not only would there be peace and quiet but the night sky would be unaffected by the pollution caused by modern electric lights.

Scripture indicates the reason for going into the wilderness away from people. It is, in the Christian tradition, not about meditating or breathing exercises or adopting a certain position with the body. It is to communicate with God. To do so without competing attractions.

---

[134] 1 Sam. 22:1 & 23:14.
[135] Luke 6:12-13.
[136] Matt. 14:23.
[137] Matt. 14:13.
[138] Mark 1:35.

We all should need times like this especially in our noisy world. A regular day free from looking at or listening to electronic devices would be a start. Not least giving a freedom from bad news. But take the hard case. How, says the tired mother with three boisterous toddlers, can I fit silence and a time to think into my day? It was all right for those men. Moses was married and had kids but I am not so sure about the others. And as for my husband helping, that is another story.

There are practical issues. Yes, you may not be able easily to escape into the remote parts of Scotland by yourself, so you have to set aside a place and a time in your own house. But how much time do you need to talk to God or to listen to God? Half an hour is best, but five minutes will do. Usually early morning or night time. Every day.

A traditional recommendation was to teach children to kneel by their beds for family night time prayers.[139] This beautiful and pious custom is probably disappearing to the detriment of us all. Introducing moments of silence in that routine can be valuable. Teaching children silence. Buddhist children are brought up this way. An escape from being busy and a release from noise and electronic devices may have many benefits for our lives: for health as well as for spirituality.

---

[139] Christopher Jamison, *Finding Sanctuary* (2006) pp 42-49.

It is not good Christianity always to be busy. St. Benedict realised this when he wrote his Rule on the conduct of monastic life. He said that idleness was the enemy of the soul. But he also limited the daily hours of work for monks so that there was time to read, to think and to be silent. The good and contented life is about balance.

The main aim of the Christian life is to get closer to God. The status quo is not a viable option for a practising believer. This is why communication with God is so important. The best time to do that is away from crowds and human noise. This was the experience, in communities quieter than ours, of Moses, Elijah, Jesus and others. It is a rather foolish Christian who would think that they do not need the same.

11. John the Baptist

Luke 3:2-14.

For the modern Christian John the Baptist can be one of the most puzzling figures in the New Testament. There cannot be any doubt about his importance. The first three Gospels tell us of the birth, ministry and death of this strange figure. In that sense we know more about him than anyone else in the Gospels apart from Jesus. More about his life than any of the Apostles including Paul. More than Mary, the mother of Jesus, or Joseph. We cannot be intended to ignore John, or treat him just as some link between the Judaism of the Old Testament and the covenant of the New. Jesus said that of those born of women no one was greater than John.[140] The highest praise he gave any human being.

One week ago last Friday, on 24th June, millions of Christians around the world celebrated the birth of John the Baptist. It was a principal feast day in the Roman Catholic Church, the Orthodox Church, the Lutheran Church and the Anglican Church. So for about one and a half billion Christians the date was important. The date chosen is six months before Christmas as John was about six months older than Jesus. Unusually it is the birth, not the death, of John which is

---

[140] Luke 7:28; Matt. 11:11.

commemorated unlike the practice for all other saints except the mother of Jesus (although his death is also remembered). We do not have feast days, festivals or commemorations throughout the year relating to particular saints but why are we told about John and what possible relevance can he have for the lives of people in this church this morning?

One obvious answer is his practice of baptism. This was somewhat different from the Jewish practice of *mikveh* which was, and is, total immersion for purification while naked in a specially constructed bath in a synagogue or, for the wealthy, in the private dwelling of the priests. This purification was done frequently, for example, after menstruation or before entering the Temple.[141] It is thanks to John that we have baptism although his baptism was linked to forgiveness from sin.[142] This does not obviously fit our practice of a once and for all baptism of infants, as well as adults, in church but without full immersion.[143]

---

[141] For more detail see Lev. 15 and Num. 19.

[142] see also Acts 2:38-39.

[143] It is not, however, said in the Gospels that John baptised a person once only. To read the Christian practice back into John is to be anachronistic: Joseph A. Fitzmyer, *The Gospel According to Luke (I-IX)* (1981) p.460. A contrary view is in James D. G. Dunn, *Jesus Remembered* (2003) p.357. It is plausible that John's baptism was derived from the Essenes

The theology of baptism is amazingly complex and Churches disagree widely on the theory and in their practices. There have been astonishing variations over the years. For example, some early churches in the East linked baptism to an oath of celibacy. This somewhat limited the use of the practice![144] In very modern usage, it seems that some members of the baptismal party may be more interested in imbibing spirits of a type different from the Holy Spirit. I guess that most regular Church goers concentrate on the joy of the ritual which their Church adopts. But the whole subject needs a separate sermon.

I want to discuss what other messages there are for us in the life and the ministry of John. The most obvious image is of this early hippy living in the desert dressed in strange clothes and with a weird diet. Mark records: "Now John was clothed with camel's hair, with a leather belt around his waist, and he ate locusts and wild honey."[145] His dress of camel hair was an odd choice for a Jew because a camel was an unclean animal.[146] Camel hair is rough unless the soft undercoat is used. It is, however, good at protecting from heat

---

practice of purification; *The Complete Dead Sea Scrolls in English*, trans. Geza Vermes (rvd. ed. 2004), p.398.
[144] Stuart G. Hall, *Doctrine and Practice in the Early Church* (2nd ed. 2005) p.45.
[145] Mark 1:6.
[146] Lev. 11:4.

and cold. He was rejecting normal Jewish rules in many ways and possibly scratching a bit.

There has been a lot of ink spilled about his diet. But locusts were the only insect a Jew could eat,[147] and they may have been a valuable source of protein and minerals including calcium. But whatever his food, and he would, for example, have had to obtain vitamin C from somewhere, there are messages behind it.

The first is faith in God. Just finding your food, with no concern for tomorrow's food. It is the message about not worrying about the future.[148] The point of his diet, or at least the mention of it in Scripture, was to emphasise moderation and simplicity. As Paul said in Philippians 3[149] there are those who are enemies of Christ. "Their end is destruction; their god is the belly." Originally in the early Western Church gluttony was mentioned as one of the seven deadly sins.[150] But you will rarely, if ever, hear a sermon on gluttony nowadays.

John was ascetic. In effect he was a monk, which originally was a word which comes from the Greek *monos* meaning alone. John was not a hermit, at

---

[147] Lev. 11:20-23.
[148] Matt. 6:25-34; Luke 12: 22-31.
[149] v.19.
[150] See also Prov. 23:2; 23:20-21; 28:7.

least in the last stages of his ministry. He was visited by crowds. But, so far as we know, he did not live in a community like modern monks. His life style was simple. He rejected the philosophy that money and wealth are signs of rewards from God or necessary to relate to God.

The whole issue was summarised by Calvin in a way that may surprise anyone who thinks he was the great Puritan. He wrote: "And we have never been forbidden to laugh, or to be filled, or to join new possessions to old or ancestral ones, or to delight in musical harmony, or to drink wine. True indeed. But where there is plenty, to wallow in delights, to gorge oneself, to intoxicate mind and heart with present pleasures and be always panting after new ones - such are very far removed from a lawful use of God's gifts."[151] The proper Christian message is one of moderation and balance.

John lived, preached and baptised in a desert, the translations say. The Greek word was *eremos* which can be translated as "wilderness". The Greek can also imply a place of solitude. The Judean desert is hot and rocky, and living there would be impossible, although in a few places there are rivers, trees, shrubs and animals. Prior to the 20th century the word "desert" in English meant sparsely populated that is - "deserted". The

---

[151] *Institutes of the Christian Religion,* Bk.111. Ch. xix.9.

wilderness was not that isolated - crowds could get to it. The point about John, or Jesus, going to the "desert" was to get away from people and the trials of daily life. For the purpose of prayer or meditation. We need, from time to time, to concentrate on our own internal spirituality and its growth. To get closer to God. It would not make sense for all of us to become monks or nuns, but the modern equivalent of going into the desert or wilderness can be going on retreat. Any congregation can organise its own retreats, which can take many forms. But it does require people to realise that that is what they need.

In the teaching from Luke, John deals with economic sins. Those with two cloaks or food should share with those who have not. A modern view would be that they should pay a fair amount of taxes. The tax collector should not overcharge. The soldier should not abuse power by extorting money - like the traffic police in some countries today. John did not say that someone must not be a tax collector or a soldier. They were probably Jews working in the service of the Roman colonisers, but John was not trying to upset the social order. Incidentally "tax collector" is a usual but, arguably, a misleading translation. The word used in the Greek can mean toll collector. Someone normally employed in local toll houses.[152] They had the power to demand more

---

[152] The word used is *telonai*: Fitzmyer, *op. cit.* p.470.

than was due. Nor was John an early trade unionist. The soldiers had to be content with their pay. John's concern was with overcharging or unfair practices or the wealthy overlooking the needy. A message which is still relevant.

There is a model of humility; that is being grounded in reality, in the "humus" or earth. Not over estimating a place in life, nor underestimating it. John was a man of very strong opinions which he expressed quickly, Few today would address those who came to hear them preach as snakes or "a brood of vipers" with its allusion to the serpent who tempted Eve. Also his criticism of the marriage of Herod and Herodias led to his death. John was not meek. But John accepted a secondary role. He said that he was not worthy to carry the sandals of Jesus or untie their thongs.[153]

We live in a society which values a winner. Coming second, let alone fourth, can be viewed as failure. Our TV screens are full of competitions which is not always the best message for the young, especially if there is humiliation of those who fail - those who do not make it to the next round or to next week's programme. This is one of the sad aspects of modern life. We do not value enough those who try but who will never be the best. Actually that is most of us.

---

[153] Mark 1:7; Matt. 3:11; Luke 3:16.

All of us, especially "winners", build on others. Many a great person has arrived at their peak because of the efforts of those who have gone before.[154] Those who, unlike John, are not named or honoured. God needs those who labour so that another may triumph. We can serve God even when we have a humble life style and a lowly status in society.

If we are to attract people to Christianity we have to tell them good stories. The elements around Herod and his incestuous marriage to Herodias is another episode. John's life had it all. Religion, sex, politics and a gory murder. There were good guys and bad guys. There were strong visual scenes fit for a Hollywood movie. You can speculate on who you would cast for the various parts. The holy Jewish priest Zechariah, his righteous wife Elizabeth, Mary, the mother of Jesus, who visited the pregnant Elizabeth, the seductive Salome, the scheming Herodias, the superstitious and cruel Herod and, of course, John and Jesus. What a cast! If a Church could write the screen play it might make a fortune.

The people to feel sorry for in the story are Zechariah and Elizabeth. They were intensely religious. Zechariah was a priest. He prayed for a child although he and his wife were getting on in

---

[154] See William Barclay, *Commentary on Matthew* vol 2, p.8 and his example of the lamp lighter.

years. His prayers were answered. He was told, by the angel Gabriel no less, that the child would be filled with the Holy Spirit and turn many to God. They must have been delighted. But God can have surprises in store. One doubts if his parents wished for a son who overturned the old Jewish practices and made the Jewish priesthood irrelevant for many. A desert eccentric who carried out a strange form of baptism in a sometimes muddy river. If they lived to see this they must have wondered as parents - where did we go wrong? God answers our prayers but maybe not in the way we expect.

So John can teach us about moderation in our lifestyle, about treating others fairly, about the need to be alone to communicate with God, about humility and about expressing our religious views strongly to others. In the end that is quite a list. Mark records that "people from the whole Judean countryside and all the people of Jerusalem" went to him.[155] He was the celebrity of his day and his death would have been the local equivalent of headline news. Jesus viewed him as the greatest. We would be wise to reflect on that.

---

[155] Mark 1:5. Repeated in Matt. 3:5.

12. Why Do We Pray?

Mark 14:32-42.

In our four Gospels there are over 40 passages which refer to prayer, mainly in Matthew and Luke. If you are interested in statistics the number of references to prayer in the whole Bible is about 645. Dr. James Strong and his colleagues counted them over a hundred years ago without the aid of a computer.[156] So there is a lot of material on prayer. Too much for one sermon. Today I want to concentrate on the circumstances in which Jesus prayed, because if anyone can teach us about prayer to God it must be the Son of God.

In the text from Mark, Jesus is in dire straights. He was distressed and agitated. No wonder, if he was about to be scourged and crucified. Jesus prayed. He often prayed. For example after he had been baptized,[157] and after he had cured the leper and other diseases[158] and just before selecting the apostles.[159] It was when he had finished praying that, according to Luke,[160]

---

[156] James Strong, *The New Strong's Expanded Exhaustive Concordance of the Bible* (2010) using the King James version of the Bible.
[157] Luke 3:21.
[158] Luke 5:16.
[159] Luke 6:12.
[160] Luke 11:1.

one of the disciples asked him to teach them to pray: and the result was the Lord's Prayer. That, incidentally, has some Jewish origins.[161] The first three phrases reflect the Jewish Kaddish, the three middle phrases the Amidah and the conclusion we use is from 1 Chronicles.[162] It was not invented from scratch by Jesus. It is a compilation. Just as modern preachers have been known to produce a prayer by pasting and cutting from several existing sources. The name given to the prayer today by Jewish or Messianic Christians is in Hebrew- *tefillat ha talmidim*. *Tefillat* is "prayer". *Talmadim* is "disciple". The disciples' prayer. In some ways a more meaningful or accurate description than "the Lord's prayer", a title Jesus never gave to it.

Often Jesus prayed on his own. He is recorded as going up a mountain by himself[163] or going to a deserted place.[164] He would pray at night when he would be alone.[165] He told us to go into our room, and shut the door and pray to the Father in secret.[166] Incidentally, the command to go into your private room, or closet, as the King

---

[161] The issue is complicated because of doubts about the dates of the relevant Jewish texts. See Andrew B. McGowan, *Ancient Christian Worship* (2014), p.187.
[162] 1 Chron. 29:11.
[163] Matt. 14:23; Mark 6:46; Luke 6:12.
[164] Mark 1:35: Luke 5:16.
[165] Mark 1:35; Luke 6:12.
[166] Matt. 6.6.

James Bible called it, is also found in Isaiah.[167] If only teenage children knew that they had biblical authority for their occasional isolation.

The reason for going away by himself? In Jewish theology prayer was a communion with God. Meditating in his presence, perhaps without words. Maybe for a long time. The downside of group prayer, as in a Church, is that intimacy with God is more difficult.

But in the Garden of Gethsemane it was different. Jesus wanted to pray with Peter, James and John and was only a little distance from them. A prayer group. And they were there to pray, which is why he chided them when they fell asleep. Not only is Jesus himself praying but he instructed the disciples to pray. To pray for themselves, not for him, interestingly.

Three times the disciples were woken up. Mark is a great storyteller, the best of the Gospel writers, and he used the technique of triple repetition - everything in threes - for emphasis and so that both the raconteur and the audience could remember.[168]   Other   examples,   restricting ourselves to the Easter story, is Peter's denials, or Pilate's   questions   to   the   crowd.   The   same

---

[167] Isa. 26:20.
[168] Henry Wansbrough, *Introducing the New Testament* (2015) p.74.

technique used by storytellers throughout the ages as in Little Red Riding Hood, the Three Bears, The Three Little Pigs and other fairy tales which you may remember. And, of course, Mark was setting down what was originally a story passed on, again and again, by word of mouth. So it may be that Jesus woke the disciples only once as Luke suggests.[169] A more realistic scenario. But we need not worry about precise historical accuracy of eye witnesses or story tellers. As so often the versions of the Gospel writers do differ. Anyone who thinks otherwise should buy a Synoptic Gospel Comparison.[170] But when the Gospels agree we should take special note. The first three Gospels all say that Jesus was bothered by the failure of the disciples to pray. It must have mattered. Would nothing have changed, prayer or no prayer? It cannot be.

But, of course, in this case, God's will was done, so far as Jesus was concerned and, despite Jesus's prayer, he was crucified. Yet elsewhere in the Gospels we are told "Ask, and it will be given you."[171] or "Whatever you ask for in prayer with faith, you will receive."[172] So what is going on? We all know that when we pray for a loved one who is

---

[169] Luke 22:45-6.; cf. Matt. 26:40-45, who follows Mark.
[170] e.g. Burton H. Throckmorton, *Gospel Parallels* (5th ed.1992)
[171] Luke 11:9.
[172] Matt 21:22.following Mark 11:24.

seriously ill, sometimes they might not recover. It appears that our prayer is not answered.

This is a case when common sense should tell us that we cannot take too literally every word in the Bible. Jesus said that by prayer we could lift up a mountain and throw it into the sea.[173] We need to look at the message behind the illustrations and appreciate the figurative way of speaking which a Rabbi might use in teaching. Just as, for example, today when someone says a mountain was made out of a molehill, they do not mean that that literally happened. Any other way of interpretation produces absurd results and Christians should not be people who leave common sense at the door.

God will answer our prayers, that is the promise, but it will be God's answer; not ours and in God's time. Study the story of Abraham as one of the first examples in the Bible. Ask and we will receive but we may not receive what we ask. Say a child says to his father that he would like an ice cream. Jesus's examples in Luke 11[174] were the healthier diet of fish or an egg. A loving father might grant the request. All parents, and grand parents, sometimes do. But when the demand is for a second or third ice cream, the wise father

---

[173] Mark 11:23; Matt. 21:21. Likewise with transplanting a mulberry tree into the sea: Luke 17:6.
[174] vv 11 to 13.

may say "No." Then, perhaps, try to give the child a lesson on greed or patience or diet. A teaching which the young child might not appreciate.

The theologian Professor Arthur Gossip gave the example of what he would have prayed for if he had been in Jerusalem during the hours when Jesus was betrayed. With passionate insistence he would have prayed, for Christ's sake, that God would burst in and save Jesus. If that prayer had been granted where would our poor and desperate world be today?[175] What seemed like utter ruin and desolation, the destruction of a life and a ministry, was seen differently by God.

Prayer has many facets, as the psalms show: many of them are prayers. They are prayers because, by and large, they are words addressed to God rather than telling us a story. Their extraordinary importance is that they show us how to speak to God.[176] It is why some churches concentrate on singing psalms, from Roman Catholic monasteries and convents to fundamental Protestant churches.

As the Psalms show we can praise God. We can ask forgiveness of sins. We can seek help. We can lament -a psalmist's word, or, if you prefer, moan. We can wait for guidance from God. Like

---

[175] A J. Gossip, *Experience Worketh Hope* (1944) p.18.
[176] John Eaton, *The Psalms* (2005), p.3.

any conversation with a loved one it can take several forms. If, on the other hand, a relationship is one sided and one party always does the talking, and all the demanding, the relationship will be in trouble. If your idea of prayer is always "Lord, get me out of here", you are heading for disappointment.

The problem comes from the Latin which is at the base of the word "prayer", a word meaning to ask or to petition. This has misled Christians. More valuable is the Hebrew word for prayer which we have already used- *tefillah*. It has a very surprising origin in a word which means to judge; and a judge can intervene or interpose a decision. But *tefillah* is the reflexive form and means to judge oneself! Prayer is about examining oneself? There may not be many members of this congregation who have ever thought of prayer in that way - the Jewish way. But Jesus was a Jew who mainly addressed Jews. Prayer is examining your own thoughts, your own worries and placing them before God. Which is why confession of sins can be part of prayer. Yes, there is an element of intercession, as a judge can intervene - but in essence prayer is asking God to teach us. To learn what God wants.

Take a practical example. A member of this congregation whose spouse is seriously ill. Nor, despite prayer, does the condition improve. Things are getting worse. The terrible, inevitable, desperately undesired, prospect seems obvious. So what does prayer achieve? The love of God envelopes the person who prays with faith and humility. There is given a courage and strength to deal with what has to be faced. Prayer changes the person who prays. That is what happened to Jesus in the passage from Mark. Also Matthew records Jesus starting his prayer grieved and agitated. After prayers he was calmer. "Get up, let us be going. See, my betrayer is at hand.[177]" Yes, Jesus was calmed by prayer: how much more can that apply to us. Luke says, in a disputed passage which is not in all manuscripts, that an angel gave him strength.[178]   Some theologians have had problems with the idea that Jesus needed the assistance of an angel, which may explain the absence from some manuscripts.[179] That may not worry us. Any angel must have come from God who had not deserted Jesus, but was answering his prayer. Jesus also died so quickly on the Cross that Pilate could not believe it.[180]

There is no doubt that prayer can improve your relationship with God when you discuss with

---

[177] Matt. 26: 37-46; see also Mark 14: 33-42.
[178] Luke 22:43.
[179] F. L. Godet, *Commentary on Luke* (1981) p.475; Joseph A Fitzmyer, T*he Gospel According to Luke (X-XXXIV)* (1985) p.1443. The Nicene doctrine of the Trinity may have been an issue.
[180] Mark 15:44; the reason could be the severity of his beating or divine intervention.

Him yourself and your problems. Especially when you do it frequently. There have been many theories about the nature of prayer and theologians have differed on the subject. One view is that prayer is a conversation with God. It is like the ladder that in Jacob's dream connected the earth with heaven.[181] A two way route, as ladders are. Thoughts, like angels, ascend and descend.

But how does all this work when we pray for others? The Letter of James tells us that we should pray for the sick. James 5:15 says that the prayer of faith will save the sick. That may be a mental strengthening, or a spiritual saving of the soul, if not a physical healing. But if again you take a literal interpretation of the Bible you are going to have problems with James 5. There will be an issue when you become ill. You are meant, according to James, to get the elders of this church round your hospital bed, all 21 or so of them, and have them anoint you with olive oil.[182]

There are examples in the Bible of prayer for others. The Lord's prayer is in the plural "Our Father … give us" not "My Father … give me". We

---

[181] Compare Gen. 28:12 and John 1:51.

[182] James 5:14; this is not something which Jesus ever did and James may be reflecting Jewish medical practice because when the disciples cured they anointed many with oil; Mark 6:13. See also the parable of the good Samaritan - Luke 10;34. In general see Ralph P. Martin, *World Biblical Commentary*, vol 48, James (1988) pp.206-210.

are praying for each other. The present Pope, Pope Francis, when he was first appointed could startle people when he concluded an address with "Pray for me". They thought the job of Pope was to pray for them. But all preachers need to be prayed for - that is not a hint, just good theology. We all need each others' prayers.

Jesus in John 17 prayed for the disciples. Moses prayed to God for the Israelites and Exodus 32:14 states: "And the Lord changed his mind about the disaster that he planned to bring on his people." The most famous intercessionary prayer ever. Less well known is Amos's intercessionary prayers which also saved Israel.[183]

To have a good relationship with God: to speak to him and to hear him, we need to pray frequently. If a son or daughter never spoke to a father or mother it would be difficult to have a close relationship. There would be a high risk of misunderstanding when there was a communication only on the occurrence of a life crisis. In Thessalonians[184] we are told to rejoice always and pray without ceasing. That is many times a day.

---

[183] Amos 7:1-6. See also Paul's prayer for the Philippians: Phil. 1:4 & 9-11 and the instructions on prayer in 1Tim. 2:1-8. Also Col.1:3 & 9; 1 Thess. 1:2; Rom. 1:8-10.
[184] 1 Thess. 5:17; see also Rom. 12:12.

A simple three word prayer will often do. Three examples. "Jesus remember me"; "Thank you Lord" or "Lord help me." That prayer "Lord help me" is what the Syrophoenician woman said to Jesus.[185] It was the prayer that the famous American preacher Dwight L Moody taught the ragamuffins of Chicago in his Sunday School. Even people who knew little English could remember it.[186] Say it frequently: "Lord help me".[187] The Lord knows what is best for us, we do not have to tell him.[188] Nevertheless Jesus emphasised the need for us to be persistent in prayer.[189] Jesus himself prayed a lot. If the Son of God had to do that, we all need an energetic prayer life.

Our heart must also be in the words. If we read a prayer from a book, for example, there is a danger that the prayer is as mechanical as turning a Tibetan prayer wheel, or three. If we are not engaged with God we are speaking to ourselves or

---

[185] Matt.15:25.

[186] Kevin Belmonte, *A Life: D. L. Moody* (2014) p.58.

[187] One of the Desert Fathers, Macarius, said:" There is no need to talk much in prayer. Reach out your hands often, and say, "Lord have mercy on me, as you will and as you know." But if conflict troubles you, say, "Lord, help me." He knows what is best for us, and has mercy." *The Desert Fathers* (trans Benedicta Ward (2003) p.132. The early practice was to pray standing with the hands outstretched, which mimics the Cross.

[188] Matt. 6:8.

[189] Luke 11: 5-8.

to those around us.[190] The downside of some prayers in Church is that the person leading the prayers could be uttering useless words, while the congregation think about Sunday lunch. Particularly if there is a long intercessionary prayer which heaps standard phrase on phrase in contravention of Jesus's observations in Matthew 6:7. Jesus warns against what the Greek calls *battalogesete*.[191] This is difficult to translate but the meaning usually given is to avoid babbling or meaningless and mechanical repetition of phrases. Jesus also warns against the thought that we might be heard by using many words. The Lord's Prayer in Matthew in the original Greek is 58 words and said by a native Greek it takes less than 60 seconds. As Ecclesiastes 5: 2 says in the context of addressing God - "let your words be few" - a command which every preacher should read or, as Proverbs 10:19 states, "the prudent are restrained in speech" which is a phrase better used at the end rather than the beginning of a sermon. The painting by Nicholas Maes on our Order of Service[192] has an important character in the bottom right hand corner. An impatient cat. Hence its

---

[190] A point made in John Blanchard, *Major Points From The Minor Prophets* (2012) p.49.

[191] It comes from two Greek words: *battos,* meaning "stammerer" and *logos* meaning "the word by which the inward thought is expressed". Jesus also criticised the long prayers of the scribes: Mark 12:40; Luke 20:47.

[192] *Old woman in prayer*, known as *Prayer without end*; (circa 1656).

alternative title of the Long Prayer. "Get on with it" is the meaning.

Prayer is the method by which we can get guidance from God. It is a way of getting into the mind of God that is magical and precious. As the Lord said to Jeremiah: "Call to me and I will answer you, and tell you great and hidden things that you have not known."[193]

---

[193] Jer. 33:3.

13. Good Friday: Going to Paradise

Luke 23:32-43

Jesus was crucified along with two others. Who were they? The King James Bible called them malefactors, which is an accurate translation of the Greek in the language of the day. An editorial heading, which is not part of Holy Scripture, although such headings are often, arguably wrongly, read out by readers in Church, had the phrase "The Penitent Thief". This has come down to us through the ages. Modern translations use the word "criminals".[194] The Greek word in Luke is *kakourgoi*. It comes from two words - *kakos* meaning evil and *ergo* meaning work. So *kakourgoi* means evil doers or, colloquially, "bad guys". Nothing about theft. The Greek for "thief" is *kleftis,* which is quite different. And the other problem with the traditional word "thief" is that theft was not normally punished by crucifixion. The Romans used crucifixion as the method of carrying out a death sentence only for the most serious crimes against the order of the Roman State. The possibility is that both of them were serial robbers, bandits or murderers. Jesus was to be humiliated

---

[194] This is the translation in NRSV, ESV, NIV, REB and NJB. They also are unanimous in using the word "others" in the equivalent passage in John. There are variations in their translations of Matt. and Mark where "bandits" or "robbers" are the terms used.

by being labeled the King of Jews and publicly put to death alongside criminals, probably serious criminals.[195]

What a contrast we have between the two of them. Both were beside Christ. Both were in the same position of facing painful death. Both were serious sinners: they probably had harmed a lot of people. One mocked Jesus. He did not believe. He died in his sins. The hard man, dying as he lived. Unrepentant, unbelieving. Feeling superior.

The other believed and was saved. And note what he believed. He asked Jesus to remember him when Jesus came into his Kingdom. In other words he knew that Jesus was going to his Kingdom, without a deep theological knowledge of what "Kingdom" meant. He did not have to decide whether he preferred the Roman Catholic view of Kingdom compared with the Protestant view. Or whether he preferred George Ladd[196] to the theology of Norman Perrin.[197] He would never have been to a communion service and possibly would not have had a Christian baptism. Nor, of course, did he know about the resurrection.

---

[195] Any idea that they were the simplest of petty thieves is likely to be romantic nonsense. See Matthew Harmon, *Philippians* (2015) pp. 217-2218 and authority there cited.
[196] *A Theology of the New Testament* (ed. D. A. Hagner, 1994).
[197] *The Kingdom of God in the Teaching of Jesus* (2012).

The criminal did not make a long prayer. He merely acknowledged God and Jesus. But as Paul wrote in Romans 10:13 "Everyone who calls on the name of Jesus is saved."[198] "Jesus remember me" could be the shortest and most effective prayer you ever make. And as Jesus indicated in Matthew 6:7 our Father likes short prayers. The criminal did not even ask Jesus to save him so that he could go to Heaven or ask for forgiveness of his sins. With humility it was enough for him that Jesus in Heaven remembered him. He did not have a high expectation.

Luke wrote in the Greek, a language which, incidentally, Jesus possibly spoke, especially to Pontius Pilate or a Roman centurion. Recent archaeological evidence four miles away from Nazareth suggests that Greek was a common second language for Jews after Aramaic.[199] Greek was the common language of most people in daily trading. The language to use to reach the widest possible audience and why the NT is in Greek. Indeed very recent scholarship argues that the evidence is now strong that Greek may have been the first language of Jesus and the disciples.[200] This is bound to be disputed, biblical scholars

---

[198] Citing Joel 2:32.

[199] Craig A. Evans, *Jesus and His World: The archaeological evidence* (2012) pp 20-22 and 41.

[200] G. Scott Gleaves, *Did Jesus Speak Greek? The Emerging Evidence of Greek Dominance in First Century Palestine* (2015).

being what they are, but, if true, it would mean some re-writing of traditional views. What is certain is that Greek was the spoken language of many Romans at the time. Latin was used for written communication, including on memorials.

What Luke wrote and what Jesus just might have said to the criminal was: *"semeron met emou ese en to paradeeso"*: literally "today with me you will be in the paradise". The word *semeron* "today" is theologically significant but I pass over it in this sermon.

There are two small words: *met emou* which mean "with me": Arguably two of the most important words in Christianity. Jesus did not say to the criminal simply: "you will be going to Paradise". "Paradise" -*"parádeisos"* -is an unusual word occurring only three times in the New Testament. It is derived from a Persian word meaning walled garden or a park. So by itself going to Paradise might have meant being re-incarnated as a park keeper, perhaps in a celestial Garden of Eden,[201] with a hi viz waistcoat, no doubt shining extra bright. But there was much, much, more. Jesus said *"met emou"*, with me. He was going, with Jesus, where Jesus was going. And Jesus we can be sure was going to his

---

[201] Liddell and Scott's *Greek-English Lexicon* states that is an Eastern word used in the Septuagint for the garden of Eden.

heavenly Father. Where we are going. But the criminal who was scornful and unrepentant and unbelieving? He was not going to Paradise. And in our modern society there are many like him. They can hear the message of Jesus and turn away. One person is completely indifferent to Christ. Another prays and, for his or her part, remembers Jesus.

But before it seems all too easy for most in this congregation, who do remember Jesus, think what else the believing criminal did. As Matthew's Gospel makes clearer, there were passers by who derided Jesus shaking their heads. "You who would destroy the temple and build it in three days, save yourself! If you are the Son of God, come down from the cross." Also he was mocked by the chief priests, the scribes and the elders who had come along to see the bloody results of their hate.[202] If we had been there would we, in Stuart Townend's words in our hymn,[203] have heard our mocking voice call out among the scoffers?

It may be more likely than we think. Those who come to Church are often sincerely religious people who can be hostile to anyone who tries to upset the foundations of their beliefs. But Jesus did that to the Jews, for example, by his attitude to Pharisees, to the Sabbath and to sinners, by

---

[202] Matt 27:39-43.

[203] Stuart Townend, *How deep the Father's love for us* v.2.

challenging Temple administration and by the way he claimed to speak for God. The opposition to him would have come not just from a few priests anxious to protect their status but from the ordinary people who went to the synagogue. Those who saw Jesus subverting the established order and taking people away from the true religion. The troublemaker had to be eliminated.[204] There would be many people who were glad that he was being put to death. After all Deuteronomy says that God commands us to purge the evil of false prophets from our midst and obey the voice of God only.[205] If we had been good Jews, would we have thought Jesus a false prophet, contradicting the traditional teaching? But while all around were shouting their scorn, one man on a cross, in that hostile atmosphere, spoke up for Jesus. That makes it even easier to understand that Jesus knew that he really believed.

To attend a Church you do not have to believe in God or Jesus. Or you can have doubts. All are welcome. But how many of those of us who consider ourselves strong believers, today speak

---

[204] A point made in Raymond E. Brown, *Crucified Christ in Holy Week* (1986) p.12.

[205] Deut. 13:1-5; see also Lev. 24:16 on the blasphemy which was charge against Jesus. The charge against Paul in Corinth was that he was persuading people to worship God in ways which were contrary to the law - Acts 18:13. See also the accusations against Stephen in Acts 6:11 which led to his death.

up for Jesus in public when all around are mocking him? Are you a disciple who proclaims the good news?[206] Do you remain silent with the thought that private belief is sufficient? Do you wish not to upset others or get into an argument? Not even telling someone with joy that you are going to, or have been to, church.

In 2 Corinthians 5[207] Paul wrote that we are ambassadors for Christ. An ambassador is a stranger in a foreign land. He or she is someone who speaks up for their native country and represents it. Here as Professor Willie Barclay said[208] "is the Christians' proud privilege and almost terrifying responsibility. The honour of Christ and of the Church are in the hands of each one of us." Speaking up for Christ in modern British society can have adverse consequences particularly in certain employment. But the comfort is in the familiar words of the Sermon on the Mount. "Blessed are you when people revile you and persecute you and utter all kinds of evil against you falsely on my account. Rejoice and be glad, for your reward is great in heaven ..."[209]

As we come to our minutes of reflection and silent prayer, I finish with a question. When your

---

[206] cf.Mark 16:15.
[207] v.20.
[208] *Commentary on The Letters to the Corinthians.*
[209] Matt. 5:11.

wee hour comes, when you see Jesus,[210] will you with a contented heart, be able to declare to him that you proclaimed him Lord to others, to others who despised him and who reviled you?

---

[210] Rev. 22:4.

14. Easter Day: The hope of the resurrection

John 20:1-10 and 19-29

Despite the fourth commandment we worship on Sundays, not Saturdays - the Jewish Sabbath. As the early Christians did, although because of the culture they lived in they probably had to worship in the evening after a day's work. Paul in Troas, now on the west coast of Turkey, spoke until midnight with lamps in an upstairs room and a young man sinking into a deep sleep and falling from the window.[211] They had an enthusiasm for worship and hearing the Good News, and daily prayers,[212] which we need to re-capture. Not that I am suggesting that we have weekly midnight services. But we have to thank Emperor Constantine on March 7th, 321 AD for making Sunday a public holiday.[213] For making it easier for us.

We meet today on the first day of the Jewish week, which was when, according to John, Mary Magdalene went to the tomb and saw that the stone had been removed. And on the evening of

---

[211] Acts 20:7-9; of course, there may have been a special reason for staying up late to hear Paul.

[212] Andrew B. McGowan, *Ancient Christian Worship* (2014) Chap. 6.

[213] Paul Bradshaw, *Early Christian Worship* (2nd ed. 2010), pp.83-84; *Codex Justinianus* 3.12.2.

that day, Jesus appeared to the disciples. We celebrate the resurrection every Sunday not just once a year. But today is the Sunday of Sundays, - a day when the Church should use all its powers to show joy and splendour and solemnity. As Paul said in 1 Corinthians 15 "If Christ has not been raised, your faith is futile ..."[214] We should all, as he mentioned in his letter to the Philippians, want to know Christ and the power of his resurrection.[215]

Jesus had been crucified and buried. Buried, with Pilate's permission, because the Roman practice was to leave crucified bodies to decay on the cross as a warning to others. The popular phrase following the views of Augustus Caesar was "Food for the Crows". What was left would later be destroyed and scattered. No martyr's grave or tomb allowed. The final humiliation.[216] Possibly the fate of the two others crucified with Jesus although it may be that the Temple authorities were allowed to follow the Jewish practice of burial on the day of death.[217]

---

[214] v.17.

[215] Phil. 3:10.

[216] Most internet sites repeat the usual stories about Jewish practice. This was a Roman execution. A good source is on infidels.org/library/modern/peter_kirby/tomb/roman.html

[217] During the Passover was a sensitive time and it may be that the Jewish practice of quick burial was respected: Deut. 21:22-23. See Craig A. Evans, *Jesus and his World* (2012) pp.128-130. This and other issues such as whether Jesus was allowed the dignity of a loin cloth are unknown. Pilate

After a hasty internment a Jew could do nothing with the tomb on the Jewish Sabbath, from a few minutes before sunset on the Friday until the Saturday evening. Around dawn on the Sunday, at the first available daylight, Mary went to the tomb. For all anyone knew the dream of a Messiah had ended in an early and extremely painful death of an itinerant preacher and healer. Deserted by most of his male disciples, terrified of reprisals. All that remained was for family and friends, mainly women it seems, to mourn, to tend the burial place and, indeed, to complete the burial rituals with perfume. At this point the story took a most startling, world shattering, turn. Mary found that the heavy round stone had been moved from the entrance. According to Matthew's Gospel this was done by an angel she saw.[218] Jesus's body had disappeared.

But why had the stone been moved? To let Jesus out? No. Later in the day he appeared to the disciples who were behind locked doors. Whatever the nature of his resurrected body he could pass through walls. God did not need to move the stone, except for one purpose. It was to let Mary in. To let us know that Jesus had risen.

---

was, though, taking the risk of a creating a martyr's tomb. The fact that no place was ever venerated by early Christians as the last resting place of Jesus is highly significant.
[218] Matt. 28:2.

But more had to happen or the conspiracy theorists would have had a field day and some still do. Bodies are never resurrected. Had the body been stolen? But the linen wrappings and cloth were lying as if they covered a body. There were not likely to have been left like that by grave robbers. Have you ever had a burglary? Had Jesus really died? But Matthew's Gospel records his side had been pierced with a spear to make sure he was dead. Probably piercing a lung and his heart, producing water and blood. And Roman soldiers knew about death and how to use a spear. Nevertheless none of that would have satisfied the sceptics. Which is why we have, in passages we did not hear read today, angels who spoke to Mary and also Jesus appearing to Mary in the garden.

Matthew has the story of Jesus appearing to Mary Magdalene and "the other Mary" and what seems a very curious response: "and they came to him, took hold of his feet, and worshipped him."[219] Why taking hold of his feet? A possible explanation is that it is a common feature across cultures that ghosts do not have feet.[220]

And then, as we did hear, Jesus came into a locked room, to the disciples, except Thomas. Doubting Thomas was like some of us. There was honesty about him. He was questioning and

---

[219] Matt. 28:9.
[220] Ian Boxall, *Discovering Matthew* (2014), p.169.

prepared to state his disbelief, despite all around him thinking otherwise. Belief is not like pregnancy. A lady is either pregnant or she is not. Belief is a state of varying degrees and we are all at some point, probably different points, on the curve.

Earlier than our text in John's Gospel, Thomas was the one who had doubted Jesus's description of heaven as being his Father's house where there were many dwelling places. And that Jesus was going to prepare a place for us.[221] He queried the way to Heaven. Forcing Jesus to make his famous statement: "I am the way, and the truth, and the life. No one comes to the Father except through me."[222]

Thomas wanted proof that Jesus had risen. And he got it. Not just seeing - but, it seems,[223] putting his fingers into Jesus's hands and side, in the presence of witnesses. In a room with shut doors, with Jesus again appearing in their midst.[224] In the end Thomas did believe. We have to be careful about the truth of early legends but the story is that he took Christianity to India, where he

---

[221] John 14:1-7.

[222] John 14:6.

[223] This is the obvious implication of the text but the careful reader will note that it is not explicitly stated that this happened.

[224] The text does not say exactly how Jesus appeared. See also Luke 24: 36-43 when he ate broiled fish, perhaps being hungry. There are many mysteries.

was martyred. For many centuries the Christians of Kerela called themselves St Thomas's Christians. And today on your computer you can watch You Tubes about present Christianity in Kerela, where the faith is more prevalent than in other parts of India.

Only John has the story of Doubting Thomas but Luke tells us that Jesus invited all the disciples to touch him and look at his hands and feet to see that he was not a ghost.[225] This is more important than we may realise. One of the problems about truly understanding the Bible is to appreciate the reaction of the original audience for which the words were intended. Luke and John[226] were probably addressing Greek speaking audiences influenced by Paul.[227]

Educated Greeks would have been familiar with the views of Homer and Plato and others that the body dissolved on death but the soul lived on as immortal. Plato in his *Republic,* written 400 years before Jesus, mentions souls after death being judged and the just going to a heaven where they meet in a meadow the souls who have gone before.[228] There was belief in life after death; and

---

[225] Luke 24:39-40.

[226] The tradition was that this Gospel was written at Ephesus, but there are uncertainties.

[227] See arguments in Raymond E. Brown, *An Introduction to the New Testament* (1997) pp.269-271

[228] Also in his famous work *Phaedo.*

in a heaven and hell. We sometimes overlook that these were not beliefs unique to Christianity and it may make us feel uncomfortable to realise that. There were also, it was thought, ghosts and spirits. But this was dramatically different. A resurrected body that could be touched? The story would have had an immediate impact on an audience imbued with Greek culture. The painting by Caravaggio[229] on our Order of Service may show one of the most significant events for the spread of Christianity.[230] But we need to know Greek thinking to understand why.

Jesus appeared several times to the disciples and also to two people on the road to Emmaus.[231] When Paul was writing to the church in Corinth he could say that Jesus had been seen by more than 500, many of whom were still alive[232] and also, of course, he appeared to Paul himself in a life changing moment. There were many eyewitnesses who, at the time, could be questioned.

---

[229] *The Incredulity of St Thomas*, 1601-02.

[230] We cannot be sure but it may be that Mark's Gospel was written in Rome for Romans and Matthew's Gospel was written for Jews in the Holy Land. The two Gospels written for the Greek speakers in between are the two which have the 'touching'.

[231] Luke 24:13-32; cf. Mark 16: 12-13.

[232] 1 Cor. 15:6.

Thomas, and a multitude of others, had the evidence but in a form which is denied to us. Malcolm Muggeridge once said that it was a pity that instead of the Dead Sea Scrolls we did not have the Dead Sea Video Tapes. But that is precisely the type of proof of many historical events, including the resurrection, which we cannot have. Good science studies the repeatable; history studies events which cannot be duplicated exactly. Which is where an examination of the texts and faith come in. Faith is relevant in this context because we want to know not just what happened but its religious significance -what it tells us about God.

Those who had tortured Jesus and put him to the most awful death thought they had solved their problem. They had won. They were still around. Jesus was gone and in the tomb. And his excruciating and public death was a deterrent to others. But they were wrong.

Whether by divine intervention or not, some of his enemies were heading for a nasty end. The fate of those who sought to harm Jesus and the disciples is not full of joy for the aggressors. Two accounts of the death of Judas has him dying with his bowels bursting open. Matthew has him committing suicide by hanging.

Herod the Great, who sought to murder the babies of Bethlehem including Jesus, died a horrible death soon afterwards. The story is told by the historian Josephus of his final illness with great pain in his bowels and worms and other matter coming from orifices in his body, and the general stench. The narration is so hideous we need to pass over the details. Amazingly Acts 12[233] mentions a similar death for his grandson Herod Agrippa, who had had James the son of John killed with a sword and had Peter put in prison. According to Eusebius, Pilate committed suicide.

No one now worships any of the Herods or Pilate. But over twenty centuries after Jesus was placed in the tomb people gather today all around the world in the presence of a Cross with prayers and praise. All those who think that their lives can only be broken and full of pain and disease and failure, and that injustice and death, terror and terrorism, are all around them, should remember the story of Jesus, the Son of God, who suffered at the hands of human beings and who had a lot of failure in his life.[234] But death did not have the last word. The resurrection message is that death has been overcome. There is a heaven, a paradise, where there are the souls of the dead: parents and grandparents, spouses and partners, brothers and sisters and sons and daughters. We do not know

---

[233] v.23.
[234] Heb. 12:3: "Consider him who endured such hostility against himself from sinners, so that you may not grow weary or lose heart."

exactly what this heaven is like, or the bodily form of those who have gone before us. But the Bible gives us clues. To use a saying, which is a favourite of N T Wright,[235] we have signposts but a signpost does not usually have a photograph of the final destination. Nevertheless, the signpost can be pointing in the right direction.

The souls of believers go immediately into God's presence. Jesus said to the penitent criminal: "Truly I tell you, today you will be with me in Paradise."[236] When Stephen was being stoned he looked up and saw heaven and Jesus standing at the right hand of God.[237] Paul in two places writes about us being at home with the Lord.[238] All this explains why, unlike our Roman Catholic brothers and sisters, in Protestant Churches we do not pray for the souls of the dead. Our belief is that they are already with God and there is nothing to pray for.

---

[235] But to produce a result quite the opposite from our approach!

[236] Luke 23:43.

[237] Acts 7: 55-56.

[238] 2 Cor. 5:8; Phil 1:23. See also the story of the rich man and Lazarus in Luke 16:19-31 which implies that Abraham was with Lazarus. This was prior to the resurrection which has other theological implications. Also there was no "soul sleep" for Moses and Elijah at the transfiguration; Matt. 17:3. A full citation of authority is in Millard J. Erickson, *Christian Theology*, (3rd ed. 2013) pp. 1079-1080.

There are some theologians who have taught that we do not go straight to God. That souls sleep until the second coming when Christ raises them to eternal life; the doctrine of "soul sleep". The work of the former Bishop of Durham, Professor Tom Wright has a version of this.[239] But it is not today main stream thinking and was actually rejected a long time ago by Calvin in the second work he published.[240] Calvin, with characteristic force, described soul sleep as the insanity of babblers.

The central theme of the resurrection is hope. One of the most important modern theological statements on hope was made in 2007 by a former German professor of theology, Pope Benedict XVI, in an encyclical Spe Salvi. It was named from Paul's declaration in Romans 8:24 -"in hope we are saved."[241] The German Protestant theologian Jurgen Moltmann in his classic book, *Theology of Hope*, emphasised that hope exists for all creation, not just for individuals. He also, at

---

[239] e.g. Tom Wright, *Surprised by Hope* (2007). In his view the souls are conscious of the love of God and Christ. Incidentally in Chap 4 there is an excellent account of the arguments as to why the resurrection of Jesus did happen.
[240] See discussion in Wayne Grudem, *Systematic Theology* (1994) pp.819-821 and Norman L Geisler, *Systematic Theology* (2011) pp. 1214-1224. The work of Calvin referred to, published in 1534, is *Psychopannachia* and available in English on www.monergism.com
[241] Or "by hope we are saved".

least in the English translation, contributed to the reputation of theologians in making a simple topic difficult.[242]

It is easier for us to rely on Paul and Timothy who referred the Colossians[243] to the hope laid up for them in heaven. Or to the writer of the First Letter of Peter who mentioned "a new birth into a living hope through the resurrection of Jesus Christ from the dead."[244] Or the Letter of Titus which refers to us being conferred with the "hope of eternal life".[245] You would not thank me if I went through all the 132 references to hope in the Bible.

Hope is what the secular culture does not give and about which it needs to hear. Hope is what we have and what non believers do not. The stone was rolled away. The tomb was empty. We look in and hope is given to us all. Christ is alive! Christ comes to bring good news to this and every age, till earth and sky and ocean ring with joy, with

---

[242] By way of contrast his classic *The Crucified God,* trans. R.A. Wilson and John Bowden, (2015) is much more approachable. See also his *The Future of Creation* (2012).
[243] Col. 1:5; there is a debate about who actually wrote this letter into which it is not possible to go here but a full analysis of views of scholars from 1792 onwards is in Paul Foster, *Colossians* (2016) pp.67-81.
[244] 1 Pet. 1:3.
[245] Titus 3:7.

justice, love and praise.[246] Jesus went to prepare a place for each of us.[247] In the words of the Psalmist we shall dwell in the house of the Lord forever.[248]

A Blessed Easter to you all.

---

[246] See Helen Steiner Rice, *Just for You* (1968) *"Seek Ye First the Kingdom of God."*
[247] John 14:2 and 3.
[248] Ps. 23:6.

15. The Joy of Being a Christian

John 2:1-12

A central text in mainstream Judaism is the Talmud. The Talmud is a record of rabbinic discussions pertaining to Jewish law, ethics, customs and history. A characteristic attitude taken up by the Talmud is that what has been created by God for people's pleasure must be essentially good. The Rabbis assumed that God wants his creatures to be joyful and it must therefore be sinful to shun physical happiness and material well-being. There are as many Rabbinic teachings against an ascetic way of life as they are against excess. Although the earliest Talmud we have is centuries after the destruction of the Temple in 70 AD, setting down the oral traditions and teachings, it reflects the culture into which Jesus and the disciples were born.[249]

Above a gate of Herod's temple were golden vines and grape clusters the size of a man. The size of a man in gold! So any Jew, like Jesus or

---

[249] Wine is mentioned several times in the earlier text *The Mishnah* e.g. *Menahoth 6.* See Herbert Danby, *The Mishnah* (1933) p.503. There is an argument that the drinking of "new wine" referred to in the Dead Sea Scrolls was unfermented grape juice, but that does not mean that practice was wide spread: *The Complete Dead Sea Scrolls in English*, trans. Geza Vermes (2004) p.31. We do, of course, have a legacy in our communion service or eucharist.

Peter or John entering the Temple was reminded of the importance in their culture, and their religion, of wine. A bunch of grapes was also on one of the most common small coins.

Some people worry about the first miracle recorded in John's Gospel. The miracle in which at a wedding feast, to which he and the disciples had been invited, Jesus, somewhat reluctantly, turned water into wine. Very good wine. Some 120 to 180 gallons of it. That is something like 800 bottles.

Jewish weddings went on for days and the whole village would be there. Also there were guests from nearby Nazareth, perhaps 5 or 6 miles away, at least Jesus and his mother and it seems his brothers. It is also intriguing that John takes the trouble to record that after the great celebration Jesus, his family and the disciples went to Capernaum, a fishing village on the Sea of Galilee, for several days, perhaps to recover; we do not know. What would you do if you had been eating and drinking for a week?

Some prefer to take an allegorical view of the story and talk of a spiritual absence followed by abundance. Some think it would have been better if Jesus had turned wine into water. If, at an early stage in his ministry, he had done that at a Jewish wedding, I suspect you and I would not be gathered here today. As Professor Willie Barclay pointed out there are certain religious people who shed gloom wherever they go. They are suspicious of joy and happiness. Few approaches have caused so much harm to Christianity. A survey of people coming out of Churches in a Scottish city concluded that most of the congregations looked as if they had just been to the dentist. Apologies to any dentists present. You can substitute another profession such as lawyers.

Think of some of the other stories about Jesus. After Matthew became a disciple Jesus had a dinner with many tax collectors and sinners along with his disciples.[250] This, Luke tells us, was a celebration, organised by Matthew (or Levi) in honour of Jesus.[251] The tax collector would have had the money to throw a good dinner party. The Pharisees were troubled that Jesus was eating and drinking and that he was always doing this instead of fasting and saying prayers, which was their image of a religious person.

It was said of Jesus, narrated in two of the Gospels, that "the Son of Man came eating and drinking and they said "Look, a glutton and a drunkard". "Drunkard" suggests he wasn't drinking mineral water and a glutton?[252] We do not know what Jesus looked like. But would someone

---

[250] Matt. 9:10.
[251] Luke 5:29 who calls him "Levi" as does Mark 2:14. Matt refers to "Matthew" in Matt.9:9. The argument as to whether they are the same or different people is inconclusive.
[252] Matt. 11:19: Luke 7:34.

realistically accused of being a glutton be very slim?

Jesus could have been what Sandy McCall Smith calls Precious Ramotswe - "traditionally built". Which, if true, and there is some slight archeological evidence for this possibility amongst Jews at the time, would be a great encouragement to those of you trying to lose weight. He might not have been the gaunt figure with his ribs showing as depicted on the cross by the imagination of centuries of artists.

The reality is that Jesus liked a party. He was being very Jewish. For example, Moses and the Israelites had a sing-song and dances after crossing the Red Sea. Exodus 15 spends 20 verses describing one song and the dancing and Miriam and her tambourine. Some party - but what would you do if you had just escaped a pursuing army?

To a Jew wine was joy. As the author of 1 Timothy makes clear we are meant to use what God has given us - all foods and wine - and that is more extensive than Judaism with its paradoxical list of prohibited foods - but in moderation and received with thanks to God. It is all part of the glory of God's creation. For the fruits of all creation thanks be to God as one of our hymns says.[253]

---

[253] Frederick Pratt Green, *For the fruits of all creation.*

The moderation is important. Who is the first drunk recorded in the Bible? It is Noah. He was found drunk and naked in his tent by his embarrassed sons.[254] He had planted a vineyard and overindulged in some of his own wine. That is the bit of the Noah story they may not have taught you in Sunday school. Nor need preachers follow the example of Luther who, before lecturing on this incident, thought he should get drunk the night before so he could speak as an expert on this wickedness.[255]

The moderation is emphasised throughout the Bible right up to The Letter to Titus. The author wants us all to be sober but especially singles out two groups who can become addicted to wine - presiding elders and older women.[256] Fascinating. Maybe "wine-o'clock" is nothing new.

There is, of course, another side to life. We have many blessings but also misery. The death of children, or own children, cancer, depression, poverty, injustice and many other ills. As Augustine said a very long time ago, no one can be exempt from death, deception and distress.[257] Most of us are happy most of the time. But we know all too

---

[254] Gen. 9:21-24.
[255] John Wilkinson, *The Medical History of the Reformers* (2110), p.18. Luther did sometimes drink to excess. *ibid*. p.16.
[256] Titus 1:7 and 2:3.
[257] *City of God* Bk. XIV 25.

well the troubles which can affect us and those whom we love. We cannot know why we have so much suffering in the midst of joy.

Viktor Frankl in his book *Man's Search for Meaning*[258] recounts how he had to give psychotherapy to Jews who were suffering after the holocaust. Where was God at that time amongst his chosen people? Of course, God was with everyone as they took their final steps into the gas chambers. But I want to approach this antithesis of joy from another direction.

At the end of the war the search was on for a vaccine against polio. The scientists tested vaccines on apes, in a procedure they might not use today. Give an ape a trial vaccine and then a jab of the polio virus. When the vaccine doesn't work, the ape suffers. Do you think, Dr. Frankl asked his patients,[259] that the apes had sufficiently advanced brains that they knew that their suffering would help the human race? Of course not, is the obvious reply. Do you think our brains are so far advanced that we must be able to determine the reason for every suffering? To answer that question would require the mind and knowledge of God.

---

[258] Viktor E. Frankl, *Man's Search for Meaning* (2004).
[259] Frankl *op. cit.* p.121.

We will all die. To a Christian death is not the end. Death is not defeat but a most joyful union with God. Cardinal Basil Hume died 16 years ago from cancer, utterly peacefully. It is not widely known, but some have privileged knowledge, that during his life this holy man suffered from depression: episodes when he was Abbot at Ampleforth and as an Archbishop of Westminster. As he wrote in his book *The Mystery of Love*[260] with a coded reference to his own struggles:

"I see this life as a period of training, a time of preparation, during which we learn the art of loving God and our neighbour, which is the heart of the Gospel message. … Death, for instance, comes to be seen as the way which leads us to the vision of God, the moment when we shall see him as he really is, and find our total fulfilment in love's final choice. The ultimate union with that which is most lovable, union with God. I call that the moment of ecstasy."

This thought was also encapsulated a long time ago in a saying of an Indian mystic[261] who believed in God: "When you were born you cried, and the world rejoiced. Live your life in such a way that when you die, the world cries but you rejoice."

---

[260] Basil Hume, *The Mystery of Love* (2000) pp.93-94.
[261] Kaber Das.

It is the promise of being a Christian that, whatever our present troubles, there is joy on earth in sharing the fruits of God's creation and, in heaven, joy surpassing anything here in this world. God and Jesus will be there. They will wipe every tear from our eyes. Death will be no more: mourning and crying and pain will be no more.[262] As the last verse of the last hymn we sing today says:

"purer, and higher, and greater will be our joy and our wonder, when Jesus we see."[263]

So please smile when you are leaving Church today.

---

[262] Rev. 21:4; Isa. 25:8.

[263] Fanny Jane Crosby, *To God be the glory, great things he has done.* She and her husband were blind which adds poignancy. See Fanny J Crosby, *Fanny Crosby's Memories of Eighty Years* (2015).